JOB
INTERVIEW SKILLS 101

THE COURSE YOU FORGOT TO TAKE

Ellyn Enisman

Published by Hudson House Publishing
Library of Congress Number: 2010926637
ISBN-13: 978-1-58776-910-8

The information presented herein represents the view of the author as of the date of publication. This book is presented for informational purposes only. No guarantee of employment is implied or given. Due to the rate at which conditions change, the author reserves the right to alter and update her opinions based on new conditions. While every attempt has been made to verify the information in this report, neither the author nor her affiliates/partners assume any responsibility for errors, inaccuracies, or omissions.

The names of clients have been changed. The names of HR managers and others whose comments and quotes are included in this book have been withheld for confidentiality purposes.

Manufactured in the United States of America

675 Dutchess Turnpike, Poughkeepsie, NY 12603
www.hudsonhousepub.com   (800) 724-1100

Preface

ongratulations! You've graduated from college and it's time to get a job and begin your career. Four years of studying, perhaps some internships, field work, and maybe a summer job or two, and now you have to go out and convince an employer to hire you. Eventually, it will come down to the interview and if you are prepared for that interview, you could beat the competition!

This book will help you do just that... get prepared, no matter what your major is.

This book is not written just for graduates entering business or finance. This book is written from a business perspective and applies to any major. Here's why. Whether you want a career in social work, teaching, engineering, fashion, graphic design, biology, psychology, or any other field, whatever company hires you is a business and will be run like a business. For example, if you are graduating with a bachelor's degree in social work, you may want to do case management in a hospital. Well, that hospital is a business and the hiring will be done the way all hiring is done, and any potential hire must be interviewed. Even in a non-profit organization there will be an interview process. Perhaps you are a graphic design major and want to work for a marketing firm or a small boutique design firm. You will be interviewed. So this book is for all new grads and students because each and every one of you needs to interview well in order to get hired.

I have spent my career recruiting, interviewing, hiring, and helping find jobs for candidates just like you and I am still surprised at how unprepared most students are when they graduate.

I've observed what a candidate can do right in an interview, and what a candidate can do wrong—and I am excited to share those experiences with you.

But don't just take my word for it!

In order to give you the best information possible, I haven't relied solely on my own experiences. This book is a culmination of seven years of research and more than 25 years of experience in staffing for my own organizations and other companies. I've interviewed many human resource directors and senior managers in the New York metropolitan area and asked them what they look for in an entry-level hire. I wanted to know what was important to them and they were willing to share with me their favorite questions and some realistic do's and don'ts in the interview process.

You'll find their honest—and valuable—advice throughout this book.

You will discover what qualities they look for in a candidate, interview do's and don'ts, and other valuable information. While each of them has their own specific advice, they all agree:

- Textbook answers don't work—that's not what interviewers want to hear.
- The interviewer wants to know you and understand how your individual experiences make you a good candidate for the position.
- They have screened countless resumes and interviewed many candidates for the position.
- They are looking for someone that stands out among the other candidates.
- When you make an impression, they remember you.

In other words, your goal is to "**CREATE A MEMORY**"!

About the Author

llyn Enisman is the founder of www.collegetoca-reercoaching.com, a professional coaching firm with a unique approach to empowering college students and recent college grads to successfully prepare for, and conquer, the job market. She has over 27 years of experience in the following areas:

- Career counseling
- Career exploration strategy coaching
- Corporate recruiting
- Employer relationship development
- Human capital management
- Human resource consulting
- Interview coaching
- Job placement
- Job search strategy coaching
- Workshops and seminars

Ellyn has held senior executive management positions in the staffing, corporate recruiting, and manufacturing industries. She has recruited, interviewed, hired, and has been instrumental in finding jobs for thousands of entry-level college grads and college students.

Ellyn has coached students from leading colleges and universities including:

Adelphi University	NYU
Bank Street College	St. Thomas Aquinas College
Bentley College	SUNY at New Paltz
Brandeis University	SUNY Albany
College of the Holy Cross	SUNY Binghampton
Duke University	Syracuse University
Dutchess Comm. College	Tufts University
Fashion Institute of Technology	University of Chicago
Fordham University	University of Maryland
George Washington University	University of Massachusetts
Georgetown University	University of Miami
Gettysburgh College	University of Michigan
Hofstra University	University of Pennsylvania
Lehigh University	University of Rhode Island
Marist College	University of Rochester
Mount Saint Mary College	University of Wisconsin
Northeastern University	Washington University in St. Louis

Ellyn lives in Dutchess County, New York with her husband Larry and their children. You are invited to contact Ellyn at Ellyn@collegetocareercoaching.com

Dedication

his book is dedicated to the memory of my mother, Iris Kraut, who showed me in her words and deeds that anything can be accomplished if you set your goal and never give up. She generously shared with me the profound wisdom of her many years, whether I asked for it or not.

My mother's belief in my ability to accomplish anything propelled me into the successful career that gave me the knowledge to write this book. She was my inspiration throughout my career and life and that inspiration motivated me through the many years that it has taken to write this book.

Although she has passed on, I live with the daily gratitude for having her in my life. I will never lose that inspiration. She would be so proud.

Thanks, Mom.

Acknowledgements

ne of the lessons I learned from my mother is that life is enriched many times over by the special people who are always in our corner supporting us and cheering us on in more ways than we can count. It has certainly been that way for me.

Thanks to my husband, Larry, for being "on call" for me 24/7, to give advice, inspiration, encouragement, and very candid feedback. My children, Bari and Jennifer, for pushing me to hurry up and get this message out. Ariel and Evan, for your encouragement. To my father Aaron, who has supported me through every up and down and whose strength, courage, sense of humor, and brilliance I can only wish to emulate. My sisters Kathi and Terri who are always reminding me how I can achieve anything.

Stewart and Dory Libes, thank you for choosing me to play a key role in your mission and vision to create and build a one-office staffing firm into a national organization. I am grateful for your support and belief in my knowledge, skill, and ability, then and to this day.

My editor, Thomas A. Hauck, thank you for your thoughtful and insightful feedback, and your love of my "wonderful book."

My web designer, Revka Stearns from Berries and Cream Blog Design, many thanks for your creativity and patience to help create www.collegetocareercoaching.com and www.jobinterviewskills101.com

The talented Adina Cucicov from Flamingo Designs, thank you for your creativity that resulted in the wonderful design and layout of this book.

To all my absolutely amazing friends, mastermind buddies, and coaching clients who have given me inspiration, motivation, and served as first readers, critics, and cheerleaders. Thank you. Thank you. Thank you.

And finally to all of my students and new grads who continuously amaze me with their knowledge, skill, ability, talent, and determination. You inspire me over and over again and have given a whole new meaning to the words, "I got the job!"

Ellyn

Table of Contents

Introduction

ou are waiting to be called in for an interview for your first job after college.

You're thinking:

> I hope I can get my palms to stop sweating before
> I have to shake the interviewer's hand.
> I'm getting really nervous.
> I hope I don't blow it.
> I hope this interview's not like the last one.
> If I hear "tell me about yourself" one more time...
> What's to tell?
> Who would want me?... I have so little experience...
> My internships were nothing special.
> How do I know what they're looking for?
> How do I know this is a job I would even want?
> I HOPE THEY LIKE ME...

What if you **could** be thinking:

> I'm really prepared and ready for this interview.
> My research tells me this company could be a
> possibility.

I am sure this interview will go even better than the last one.

If I hear "tell me about yourself" one more time, I'll know just what to say.

I am confident that the questions I ask will help me decide if this job and company meet my criteria.

If I am interested, I know how to sell myself.

I'M SURE THEY'LL LIKE ME... I HOPE THEY MEET MY CRITERIA.

If you are reading this book right now, your experiences have probably been more like scenario number one. You are not alone! In fact, after more than twenty-seven years of experience in job placement, corporate recruiting, career advisement, and interview coaching, I have observed the following:

❖ College graduates have received little or no formal, individualized interview skill training, or coaching in career exploration and job search strategy.

❖ There are few college courses that teach the real skills needed to prepare new graduates or any college student for entering the job market.

- College students and college graduates who are coached in job interview skills have a definite edge in interviewing success.

- Career services offices, although helpful and committed to students, do not have the time or staff resources to spend many hours working one-on-one with each student to help them discover and understand what really gets them the job: the knowledge, skills, and abilities they have gained from their internships, project work, and work experience, and how to articulate this in an interview.

- Most grads practice generic interview answers that don't tell the interviewer much about them and don't get them the job.

- Grads who can articulate how the knowledge, skills, and abilities they have gained apply to the job description will most often beat the competition.

After being routinely hired by students and new graduates for resume preparation, interview skill training, career coaching, and job search strategy, I have discovered that:

Many of you share anxiety, fear, frustration, and uncertainty.

Many of you are not sure what you have to offer and do not recognize how your experiences make you desirable to a company.

Think about it... For more than fifteen years, you've been immersed in academia. You know what your schedule is every day, your life is totally structured, and you know what's expected of you. Then, you graduate. You have no set schedule, your life is unstructured, and you don't have a clue about what's expected of you. All you know is you are expected to land "the great job" and anxiety sets in. You wish you had someone to help you.

With coaching, training, and through the detailed self-assessment and discovery process featured in my tool book and action planner, you could learn:

- How valuable and desirable your project work, internships, life experiences, etc., can be.

- How to speak about them to sell yourself in an interview.

- How to craft answers to questions including, *"Tell me about yourself," "What are your strengths and weaknesses," "Why should we hire you," "What makes you stand out from the other candidates,"* and *"Tell me about a time when..."*

- How to make the most of opportunities from an interview strategy and skill development program designed specifically for you, the new college graduate.

When I began coaching college students and new grads, I looked around for books that I could recommend to my clients. I found that there are plenty of books on "how to get a job," but they are geared for people who already have careers and primarily talk about how to cast your previous work experiences in the best light in order to impress interviewers. But what if you have limited previous work experience such as summer internships or part-time jobs unrelated to your career goals?

Even if you do have relevant experiences, how do you know what knowledge, skills, and abilities you have gained from them? You know what you did on the job, but no one has told you how to articulate that in an interview or helped you discover the value you bring to a company based on your experiences. There really are very few books out there written just for you—the college grad or student whose resume is still under construction, barely half a page in length, with maybe a few summer jobs and an internship or two.

So I decided to write this book because I want every college student and new grad to have the opportunity to benefit from this proven program. I know the value you have to offer. I want you to know it. I want the companies who interview you to know it.

And because... your first job really does matter.

There are times—when the economy is in a downturn, or when it seems that everyone in your graduating class is going into the same field—when desperation hits and you feel like you have to take the first job that's offered to you, even if it doesn't "feel" right or doesn't fit most of the criteria you set for yourself (if you have even thought about your criteria).

On the flipside, when the economy is booming and providing an abundance of opportunities, you want to choose the right job for the right reasons. Either way, wouldn't it be great to choose instead of waiting to be chosen? How would that feel?

Your first position does matter. It can springboard you into a career that can last a lifetime. It can also provide you with the experience, momentum, and new skills to lead you to your next position and be the first building block in the foundation for a solid career.

The Interview 101 Program

Have good reasons why you want to work for my company. Relate them to what you have learned about us before you come to the interview. I am impressed when you do your homework.

**President and CEO,
real estate development firm**

his program is divided into two parts. How you choose to participate is up to you.

Part I: Knowledge and Information

The book you are reading right now will:

- Give you the knowledge you need to prepare for the interview process.
- Help you understand the different types of interviews.
- Offer strategies to navigate the different types of interviews.
- Provide tips on how to prepare.

Part II: Tools and Action

Your personal tool book and action planner that will take you through the detailed self-assessment and discovery process. This assessment and discovery process was created by me, specifically for college students and new graduates and has brought my clients great success.

The *Tool Book and Action Planner* is a detailed manual and action guide designed to help you discover who you are and what you have to offer, and how your knowledge, skills, abilities, and experiences make you a great candidate.

You will:

- Learn interview skills that are critical in any job market that will make you competitive with the best of candidates.
- Read case studies of successful clients.
- Uncover your unique qualities, be more confident, and appropriately finesse any interview question and scenario.
- Get the tools that can enable you to draw from all your experiences to find examples to support your interview answers to whatever questions you might be asked.
- Craft personalized answers, based on your experiences, to interview questions and prepare your "30 Second Commercial," a tool every candidate must have. (see Appendix 7)

Inside the tool book is an example of a completed **assessment** along with interpretations and applications to interview questions. There is a blank assessment that you will fill out and utilize in your discovery process. The assessment is designed to help you pinpoint and define the knowledge, skills, and abilities you personally have gained from your internships, projects, work, and life experiences. The process is designed to help you craft specific answers to any interview question based on your individual experiences.

After the assessment, you will complete the **action tools** to help you find your **seven stories**. From these seven stories you will then learn how to craft your specific answers to just about any question you might be asked and the typical questions including:

"Tell me about yourself?"
"What are your strengths and weaknesses?"
"Where do you want to be in five years?"
"What are you goals?"
"Why should we hire you?"
"What makes you a good candidate for this position?"

In addition, you will find questions to ask the interviewer that I believe are essential to enhance your ability to get the job.

If you complete the entire program and do all the exercises thoroughly, you will feel more confident and your anxiety will diminish substantially. You could be ready to *Create a Memory* and get the job.

My advice?

1. Read Part I, this book, first.
2. Complete Part II.
3. Join the Inner Circle Coaching Club at www.collegetocareercoaching.com.

As a member of the Inner Circle, you can:

- Listen to telecast interviews with former clients who have succeeded.
- Participate in live coaching sessions.
- Learn job search strategy.
- Get continuously updated information.
- Hear advice from employers.
- Share stories with other students.
- Join group coaching sessions.
- Find tools to prepare for each interview.

Read on and CREATE YOUR MEMORY!

I am most impressed with grads who have worked during college, especially those who have needed to work to help pay their tuition, expenses, etc. For me that shows work ethic and commitment. Tell me about it, I want to know that about you.

In our company the key skill is the ability to multitask. When I ask about it, give me a real life example of how you are able to do it well. The example brings your skills to life and now we are having a conversation. The ability to converse in an interview is important, it's give and take and I want to get to know you as a person.

**President and COO,
global produce distributor**

2

Types of Interviews

Listen 70% of the time and speak 30% of the time. Have four or five well-crafted questions to ask the hiring manager, such as, "What are the challenges of the position?"

**President and CEO,
regional recruiting firm**

An interview... is an interview... is an interview.

Isn't it?

NO, IT ISN'T...

Everyone who is looking for a job faces an interview some-where along the way. The more you know about the interview-ing process, the more prepared you will be, and the greater the chances you will be a candidate employers want to hire. It's important to recognize that there are many different types of interviews, and you should be prepared to ace any one of them. Following are descriptions of several types of interviews, points to remember, and tips to help you finesse them:

On-Campus Company Information Session

Some companies will come to campus to do an information session. These are usually scheduled in the fall. Managers and recruiters from the company will often give a presentation about their company, and describe:

- What it is like to work for them.
- The positions they will be recruiting for.
- Responsibilities of those positions.
- What qualifications they are looking for.

- Process involved in hiring.
- Often, they will bring a recent grad, currently working for the company, who will speak about his/her experience working there.

Why should you attend an on-campus company information session? It is very important for you to attend these sessions even if you are not 100% interested in the company. Listening to the recruiters and managers will give you some insight to what companies are looking for, and their corporate culture.

If you have the slightest interest in applying to this company, then attending must be a priority! You will have the opportunity to meet the people who may be interviewing you. There is usually a question-and-answer portion of the presentation and time afterwards to personally introduce yourself to the presenters. **You must do this!** This is your chance to make a personal connection and a great first impression. Companies want to hire people who show an interest in them.

They may save the sign-in sheets or list of students who attend.

The managers and recruiters take this session very seriously. Many that I have spoken to said that they review attendance rosters and keenly have an eye out for anyone who stands out.

You can also use it as an opportunity to give them your resume and inquire what the next step will be in pursuing an opportunity with the company.

I recently spoke with a vice president from a well-known consulting firm who told me that he always checks to see if the person he is interviewing attended the campus info session and if not, he always ask why. He also reported that he gives preference to those candidates who took the time to attend.

Again, do not ignore this opportunity and if you interview with them find a place in your conversation to mention you attended.

Company Interview

Many companies send Human Resources/Campus Recruiter representatives to campus to recruit. Your Career Services office will have the dates for company interviews posted in their offices and online. In many cases, there are requirements for being interviewed such as a minimum GPA and deadlines to submit your resume in order to meet with a company. It is imperative that you don't miss the deadlines to apply for these meetings. This interview will often lead to an onsite interview and should be considered the same as an onsite interview at the company. Treat it accordingly and prepare as you would for a first interview (which you will find covered later in this book).

Career Fair Interview

This interview takes place when a group of companies come to school for a career fair put on by career services. This interview is typically brief and takes place when you approach the recruiters from the company at their exhibit or booth. It is typically a short screening process to identify possible candidates who are a match for open positions and a further interview.

Here, first impressions are everything. With interviews at career fairs being short, you have very little time to create that memory. It is important that you are well prepared with your 30-second commercial and can answer the question as to why you are interested in pursuing the company and position.

*Key Advice: Many times the on campus career fair/interview is the very first interview students have, and you may be very nervous. If this is the case for you, my advice is to pick three to five companies that you know you do **not** want to work for, and go visit them first. This is a great way to get some practice, get your feet wet, and calm your nerves. The best part is that if you say something you regret, no worries... you don't want that* *job anyway. When you are feeling more confident go see the companies you want most.*

Other Do's and Don'ts:

- Do your homework and research the companies you want to work for (covered later in this book).

- Dress professionally (covered later in this book), the same as you would for any interview.

- Get there early to get the lay of the land. Sometimes there is a map of company locations. Plot out your path so you know where you are going.

- Once inside, find a place to hang your coat. You don't want to carry it around if you don't have to. If there is no place to hang it, fold it neatly and hang it over your arm.

- Carry a leather- or vinyl-bound folio with a pad and pen inside.

- Place many copies of your resume in the portfolio.

- Do not crowd other students while they are speaking with a company representative. Stand back and give them some room.

- When it is your turn, extend your hand and introduce yourself. A firm hand shake is important even if the interviewer is a woman. But do not crush their hand.

- Make eye contact when you shake hands. To help you do this, make sure you notice the color of his or her eyes.

- SMILE when you reach out your hand and make eye contact.

- Introduce yourself: *"Hello, I am John Smith, B.S. Finance. It's a pleasure to meet you. I am interested in learning more about opportunities at your company and what you are looking for."*

- Have two or three questions to ask about the position and be ready to highlight how your knowledge, skills, abilities, and experiences meet the requirements for the position. This is where you most definitely need your 30-second commercial.

- Have two or three questions to ask in response to *"Do you have any questions for me?"* (see questions to ask employer.)

- If this is a company you are very interested in, ask what the next step is in the hiring process.

- Be aware of time. You do not want to miss out on the companies that are most important to you.

- After, ask for the business card of each person you met.

- After you leave the booth, take a minute to write something on the back of the card that will help you recall your brief encounter. The card will also tell you their title and where to email them a thank-you note.

- Email a thank-you by that evening.

The Telephone Interview

At times, employers will use telephone interviews to pre-screen potential candidates. This often happens when their recruiters are headquartered out of your area. Telephone interviews allow the employer to preselect candidates before they arrange a face-to-face interview. I always telephoned potential candidates prior to my trip into a city, because screening out the number of candidates allowed me to spend more time with the ones who were chosen for the face-to-face interview.

The telephone interview is also often used when the responsibilities of the job will require you to communicate over the phone. It may also be done because your future manager or team is based in another city and should you get the position, you will be reporting in long distance.

When scheduling your interview, make sure to:

- Ask how much time you should set aside.

- Ask the title or position of each person who will be interviewing you. This is important because the title/position of the interviewer tells you something about the focus of questions you will be getting. The HR person will be questioning for overall fit and will ask questions about your resume and some behavioral questions related to the job description. Your direct manager will ask more in-depth questions about your skills and experience as they relate to the position, and the more senior manager will question you more on overall fit and what you know about the company.

- Ask if you should call the employer, or if they will be calling you. If they will be calling you, give a phone number where you will not have any interruptions. Most often you will be doing the calling.

- Use a landline if your cell does not have reliable service.

- If using a cell phone make sure your phone is charged. You can plug in the charger while you talk so you don't have to worry about talking too long and depleting your battery.

Key Advice: If you have call waiting on your cell phone or landline, disable it by hitting *70 before dialing. This will avoid embarrassment.

Client Story

My client was interviewing with a Fortune 500 company for an account coordinator position. All of her interviews were telephone interviews. The first round was set up through a conference line and she was instructed to dial in three separate times over a period of two hours. Each time she would be meeting with a different person. After she got the notification of the interview I asked her to email the HR person who was coordinating the interview process to ask if he could tell her the positions of the three interviewers. They were account managers. So immediately we knew that they were in a direct manager position for the account coordinator position. We Googled them and found them on LinkedIn, where we found out more about what they were doing. We knew then that the interviews would be geared towards her actual experience and how it related to the job.

She was ready with her seven stories and progressed to the second round. The second round was set up with two additional people, also on the telephone. She got their positions and we Googled again and found out they were directors and one was HR and one was in the client account area. The HR person was very involved in a leadership initiative in the company and my client, because we had that information prior through our research, was able to tell the HR person that she was aware of the initiative she was involved in and ask questions about it. (Do you have any questions for me?)

About an hour after this round of interviews, my client received a call from the HR person who was coordinating the process who asked my client if she had time for one last interview. This took my client by surprise and she was so flustered she did not ask what the next interviewer's position was. I asked her to quickly email the HR person and we found out that the next interviewer was another account manager. I knew this meant only one thing. This meant that she was a serious contender and most likely she was about to be interviewed by someone who would be on her team.

My client described this interview as more of a friendly chat, which did not surprise me.

> The interviewer was checking my client out to see if they would work well together.
>
> She got the offer one week later.

What to Expect in the Telephone Interview

The interviewer may ask one or two questions, or may conduct an extensive interview. Be prepared for everything. My client Jeff called a potential employer to confirm the time for an interview. He expected an assistant to answer the phone, but was surprised when the hiring manager answered and proceeded to speak with him for half an hour. Jeff had already prepared for the interview and had his notes close by. Even though he was taken by surprise, he was able to have a successful discussion which positioned him well for the face-to-face meeting the next day. Jeff was eventually hired for that job.

As you can see by these clients stories, there are times that all interviews in your interview process will be telephone interviews. The Fortune 500 company in the previous client story explained to my client that they do this process over the phone because the team is scattered throughout the country so a great deal of work is done through the internet and telephone.

The On-Site Interview at the Employer

When you are invited to an employer's office for an interview, be sure you know whom you will be meeting with and their title/position. It is okay to ask and shows you are on top of the details. You should be clear on the position, the names and titles of the people you will be meeting with, and, if necessary, how much time the company expects the interviews to take. Many times on-site interviews are intended for more in-depth discussions.

Some points to remember about company interviews:

- **There are no guarantees**—an offer for an interview is not a job offer. It means that the company is interested in learning more about you.

- **BE ON TIME.** If something unavoidable happens that will make you late, call right away and apologize immediately. Do not wait until the end of the meeting to explain why you are late. I spoke with a vice president who interviewed a candidate who arrived late and didn't apologize until the end of their meeting. The VP said she was distracted throughout the interview and wouldn't pursue this candidate because the candidate did not handle this situation appropriately.

- **Do your homework**—before you get to the interview, find out as much as you can about the company and interviewer through the various methods discussed later in this book.

- **Bring copies of your resume**—The employer may have misplaced the one you originally provided, and/or you may be asked to see several different people during your visit. It shows you are prepared.

- **Keep a log of your visit**—write down the names and titles of everyone you spoke with and ask for their business cards.

- **Make notes on the back of each business card or in your folio.** If you were unhappy with something you said or left something out, make a note and include it in your thank you note.

- **Email each person an individual thank-you note after your visit. (samples in toolbook)**

3

Finessing Your Interview

I want to know about you. Tell me stories about your experiences with specifics.
Have good insight to your strengths and weaknesses with examples. Candidates who give me detailed answers are better. So many grads give me the typical answers, like "I am a hard worker" or "I like people." I will remember your stories and examples.

**Vice President,
manufacturer**

Competency-Based Interviewing

The majority of the interview types and styles that are described below come under the umbrella of Competency-Based Interviewing. In order to prepare and succeed, it is helpful to know the purpose and process behind this type of interviewing and how a company prepares to interview you.

How the Company Prepares to Interview You

The first step many companies take in hiring is to create a **job description**. Even now, whenever I hire candidates I do this. In addition, when I consult with companies on how to hire well, I suggest they use this template:

As a model for the job description, the company may use an exceptional performer who has been in this role. If this is a new position they may use a consensus of input from the manager and others who will interact with this position.

In building the job description, the company will look not only look at the responsibilities of the position, but also at the knowledge, skills, and abilities that are required to perform well in this position. Lumped into the abilities category will be personality traits and characteristics, which are also called "soft skills." Once the description of the responsibilities, knowledge, skills, and abilities is compiled, **core competencies** will be outlined.

Core competencies may include:

- **Knowledge:** B. S. Economics, Finance, Business, etc.
- **Skills:** Financial modeling, strong verbal and written communication.
- **Abilities:** Able to work in a team environment and work with others from diverse cultures.
- **Characteristics:** Outgoing, persistent, sense of urgency.

The above is a small sample of what usually comprises many pages. When the job description is complete, interview questions will be crafted to elicit responses that will determine if the candidate is a good match for the position. A check list may also be created, which will be completed by each interviewer in the process.

Core competencies and position descriptions usually determine which type of interview will be used, and often several types of interviews are incorporated. As an example, under "abilities" listed above, there may be a behavioral question such as, *"Tell me about a time when you were assigned to work with a team of people you didn't know previously."* In the skills area, there may be a situational question such as, *"Describe a situation where you needed to use your financial modeling skills."*

Another example might be:

Core competency: Strong customer service skills
Question: *"Tell me about a time when you encountered an irate customer."*

In summary, Competency-Based interviewing is used to determine your level of ability and how well you match the knowledge, skills, abilities, and characteristics the employer deems required to excel in the position.

Interview Styles and Strategies

After core competencies are determined and the job description is completed, the company will then build its **interview strategy**. Again, this is how I prepare and advise my corporate clients to prepare. This strategy will include how the interview is done and the type of questions that will be asked. The following is a detailed description of strategies and type of questions used.

The Behavioral Interview

This is the most common style and the one my clients are most concerned about.

This style of interview is used when an interviewer is looking to discover how you would respond to specific situations that are relevant to the job you are seeking. He or she is looking to identify the specific capabilities and skills (core competencies) you have that will enable you to successfully perform in the position. This may include technical skills, leadership ability, job-specific knowledge, and interpersonal skills. The interviewer is looking to ascertain how you responded to past challenges or situations. The belief is that past behavior is the best predictor of future behavior. Always be prepared to share a real-life scenario or experience and how you responded to it.

This is where **your seven stories** come in. Very early on in my coaching process, I have my clients determine their specific seven stories or experiences. These stories are experiences that you have had that will provide examples of your strengths, knowledge, skill, and abilities. They are experiences that you have actually had, through work, internships, school, and personal, that will be unique to you. Others may have experiences similar but no other will have your specific experiences. This is the most important piece of your interview preparation.

Why is it important? Because as a recruiter, I remember you by your stories. You will become *"the person who did the internship with the micromanaging boss in London"* or *"the person who didn't have any internships because he was needed in the family pizza business and actually ended up running the business and getting incredible management skills that really*

add value to my open position," or *"the person who unloaded trucks of thousands of small items with a team at 3:00 am for a large retail chain and had to inventory them and who therefore had my most needed skill of handling details and working in a team."*

The assessment in the tool book and action planner is designed to help you identify and elicit your experiences and craft them into your seven stories.

These stories will help you answer every competency-based question and more. They are the foundation of your responses to, *"Tell me about yourself,"* *"What are your strengths and weaknesses,"* *"Why should we hire you,"* *What makes you better than the other candidates,"* *"Tell me about a time when,"* *"Describe a situation where,"* and all the other stock questions that many interviewers ask.

Examples of behavioral questions include:

"Tell me about a time when you faced a challenge in an internship, and how you handled it."

"Tell me about a time when you demonstrated initiative."

"When have you had to gain the cooperation of a group and how did you accomplish it?"

"Give an example of time when you had to deal with a challenging personality type and how you handled it."

Recipe for a Winning Behavioral Interview, or, *How to Answer Behavior-Based Questions*

Do you have a favorite cookie, cake, or dessert that you love to eat over and over again? The reason it always tastes so great is that it is made the same way each and every time. At Thanksgiving, my family always wants my pecan pie. It always comes out great because I use the same recipe with the same ingredients, mixed in the same way every time. However, before I prepare it, I check to make sure I have all the ingredients, and whatever I don't have I go out and get. Then, I assemble every ingredient, measure, and mix, and bake, and it comes out great... same way, every time. I didn't invent the recipe, someone else did. But if I want great pecan pie, I follow the recipe because it works. If you follow my recipe for preparing for the behavioral interview to the letter, you could be very prepared and being prepared boosts confidence. This recipe can also be used for most any interview, with the exception of the case interview and brainteaser interview, covered later in this book.

STEP I: MAKE SURE YOU HAVE THE INGREDIENTS.

These are the ingredients you will need for any interview, which is why I created the tool book. You need:

- **Well-prepared resume.**
- **30-second commercial.**
- **Complete and thorough knowledge of your experiences (tool book)**
- **Your seven stories/experiences that you know thoroughly (tool book).**
- **Knowledge of your strengths and weaknesses.**
- **Job description.**
- **Your portfolio or examples of work you have done.**

  Save all of your projects on your computer. This includes spreadsheets, written commentary, papers, and anything else that you use or hand in to a professor. Some employers will ask for a writing sample. Having this material will prevent you from having to rewrite something or write something new. In addition, you want to take some of these samples of your project work with you on the interview. Set them up in your carrying case by folder and title. No doubt they will be part of your seven stories. The opportunity may present itself for you to actually show the interviewer what you are describing by taking out an example. Showing an example makes your story come alive for the interviewer. When using examples of your work from internships, remember confidentiality. Any proprietary information about the companies you worked for, including financial information or competitive information should be taken out of your examples. You can explain the reason it has been removed in your interview.

Client Story

John was interviewing for an entry-level position with a global real estate services and investment firm. He had researched the company and really wanted this job. He got the interview through networking. John grew up in a family that was in the real estate business and also began working in that business at the age of eight when his dad would wake him up the morning after a snow storm and they would go down to the properties and shovel snow. As he grew up he learned construction and helped restore and build properties. He was also fortunate enough to know how to read architectural plans and had done some demographic work. However, his articulation of what he had done needed improvement; he had a hard time finding the words and had some difficulty relating how his experience prepared him for the job he was applying for.

To prepare for our next meeting I asked him to bring examples of what he worked on. I was very excited by what I saw. He had plans of upcoming commercial real estate developments that he could speak about knowledgeably because he was working in the office during their creation. In addition, he had photos of himself with a hammer on the rooftop of a building he was helping to restore. That photo spoke volumes.

My client had been doing this work since he was 16 years old. It was clear that he was not afraid to get his hands dirty! When he explained the plans to me and told me the story behind the photo, his eyes lit up as he made the connection to how his experience prepared him for this position. He also spoke more passionately about these projects and his enthusiasm for the industry became apparent. I had him bring the plans and the photo with him in his interview. He got the opportunity to show the interviewer his work. He did very well and was invited back to meet with other members of senior management.

But soon after the interview, the position was put on hold and he was crushed. Three months later, I urged him to follow-up and—lo and behold— there was an opening. He got the job!

__Key Advice:__ Do not bring examples of your work that may have confidential information from a company you worked for. Block out that information or bring a blank copy of the spreadsheet, etc. You can then take the interviewer through it without the information. It is okay to tell them that you have taken off the numbers to protect confidentiality. The interviewer will appreciate your integrity.

To get back to our recipe—whenever I prepare my pecan pie I read the recipe at least three times.

First time: To get a feel for what is involved and just understand the overall content

Second time: To determine what ingredients I need.

Third time: To assemble each ingredient and the tools.

Preparing your recipe for the behavioral interview is no different than me making a pecan pie.

After completing Step I, move on to Step II.

A Word About Resumes

In order to get an interview you need to have a resume that speaks to the qualifications of the job and has the company recruiter say: *"This person appears to have what we need, I want to learn more about them."*

A resume must present you as a match for the position by highlighting your job-relevant knowledge, skills, and abilities. Your resume creates a picture in the mind of the interviewer. As an entry-level graduate, the interviewer does not expect you to have a wealth of hands-on experience. What they will look for are life experiences and educational achievements that provide evidence that you have the skills needed to succeed in the position. They will look for this in your internships, community service, awards, activities, and GPA. Therefore, you may need to rework your resume for each position you apply for. However, you always tell the truth on your resume. You may want to change some action verbs and bullets to align with the job description, but always, *always* be truthful.

Your resume will be one of the tools the interviewer uses to interview you, so you must be prepared to back up every detail on your resume with stories that evidence your knowledge skills, and abilities. You will no doubt be asked in-depth questions.

For more information on resumes and examples of before-and-after-resume makeovers visit my website: www.collegetocareercoaching.com

STEP II: READ THE JOB DESCRIPTION FOUR MORE TIMES.

1. Read it for content.

2. Reread it and circle, underline, or highlight the education requirements, technical skills, and the soft skills (strong work ethic, etc). I recommend color coding: Red for knowledge, green for skills, and yellow for attributes/soft skills.

3. Reread it again for further requirements such as "international travel 20%," or anything you missed and highlight those as well.

Next: *(This section is already set up for you in the tool book and an example is in the Appendix in this book.)* You will need to set up a four-column table. The four columns should labeled from left to right: Employer Needs, What I Have, Story, and Story Details. Use a table for each one of the following:

- Education
- Technical skills
- Soft skills
- Additional requirements

If you have the tool book go to the job description preparation pages and utilize the tool sheets already set up for you there.

The final step in preparing the recipe is the **fourth column, story details**. In this column you must explain how what you noted in the previous column matches the requirement. This will help you answer the question, *"Tell me about a time when..."* You should always have seven stories/experiences to draw upon to answer behavioral questions. If you do this in advance you will be prepared to handle most interview questions. The following will explain further, and the tool book through the assessment and tools/forms lays it out for you.

Review your experiences with your projects, internships, and life experiences. Choose the experiences you can use that depict the knowledge, skills, abilities, and characteristics written in the job description. These will become your seven stories so you must have seven of them. Draw on your specific experiences that illustrate your relevant strengths. Look at your project work, internships, sports, extra-curricular activities, volunteer work, and summer employment.

Be specific about what you did, and be able to explain the decisions you made.

Note: The tool book and planner includes the steps, process, and tools to prepare for this process. See Appendix as well.

Once you have chosen your stories, here's what's next:

Most career services offices use the STAR model to help students with this step, so I am going to use it here for familiarity purposes. When answering any *"Tell me about a time when..."* question the interviewer is looking for specifics as follows:

Your answers should include four parts: **S.T.A.R.**

- Situation Description: Describe the situation.
- Task/Responsibilities: What needed to be done.
- Action/Response: The actions you took and how you solved the problem.
- Result: What happened as a result of your approach.

Here is an example of a behavioral question encountered by a former client and his answer.

Client Story

Example: "Tell me about a time when you had to confront a team member who was not doing their job."

Situation: I was one of four partners in an on-campus laundry service that we all started. One of the partners was not showing up to meetings and had called each of us several times to take his shift. This was putting a lot of stress on us and our ability to get our school work done.

Task: The other three partners and I were very frustrated and angry with him, but they were not willing to discuss it with him. I knew we had to speak with him, so I volunteered to do it.

Action: I called him and arranged to meet with him in a place that insured privacy. I didn't want him to feel attacked, so I told him that the other partners and I were concerned that he was okay. He told me that he was having some difficulty keeping up with his school work, and his grades were suffering. He was finding it difficult to juggle the business and do well in school. He said he was embarrassed to tell us, as he had never had this problem before. I asked if he would be willing to sell his share of the company and he was. I though it was a

> great idea and made sense, but now I had to convince my partners.
>
> **Result:** I put my facts and figures together and pitched my idea to my partners and we bought his share. We are all still friends, and although I and the remaining partners ended up working more hours, no one was resentful.
>
> This is a thorough answer. How is it thorough?

A little earlier in this book, I described how employers create the job description and then plan the style of interview and questions. There is a purpose behind every interview question. Think about the purpose behind the question and address it. The purpose of the question used in this example is to determine how this candidate handled confrontation, conflict, and problem resolution.

The candidate's answer paints a vivid picture of his skills. He discussed it with his partner, came up with an idea, sold the idea to his partners, uncovered what the problem was that was causing the conflict, and found a way to resolve it and maintain friendships. He navigated this problem by creating a win-win solution.

As a recruiter, here is how I interpret his answer.

First, he is now the candidate that had the *"problem with his partner in the on-campus laundry business."*

Second, I now know he has empathy, negotiating skills, and critical thinking skills which problem solving always requires. He does not shy away from conflict, rather seeks to resolve it, takes initiative, can analyze a situation even though there are emotions and friendships involved, and understands how a business runs. In just one short story, I remember him and his skills, and how he/they fit my job. As a candidate he has now *"come to life for me!"* Most likely no other candidate for this job is going to have owned an on campus laundry business! I will certainly remember him through his story.

He Created a Memory.

If you want to succeed at getting the job you want you must review your seven stories and relate them to the knowledge, skills, and abilities required in the job description for every job you interview for. You will go into the interview with confidence.

Key Advice: Know your experiences thoroughly. You will get follow-up questions. For example, if I were interviewing this candidate, I might then ask, "how did you negotiate the price for buying out your partner?" This is no time to make-up stories of experiences. The interviewer will see right through it. If you put the effort into preparing this you will find many experiences to choose from and be able to answer any follow up question. The "team" questions are quite common in this type of interview because teams rarely run smoothly and there are always challenges. So think about your team experiences and you are sure to find some meaty material for your seven stories.

Client Story

A client recently came to me because he did not have any team projects in his classes and was nervous about answering questions about team work. He wanted some coaching on this. Turns out he worked for a large retail chain where he spent late-night hours unloading trucks with thousands of items of inventory. He was part of a team and at times the leader of the team. He had excellent team experiences at this company and didn't even realize it. Because it wasn't a corporate environment, he felt it was meaningless.

> **Moral of the story:** Your have many experiences. Find them in your class work, projects, summer jobs, and personal situations. Know the skills you have gotten and know your experiences and be able to explain them in the STAR format.

GETTING BACK TO THE TELEPHONE INTERVIEW… WHAT'S IMPORTANT:

- **Make sure your voicemail message is professional.** Example: *"Hi, you have reached Ellyn Enisman. Your call is important to me, so please leave your name and number and I will return your call as soon as possible."*

- **If an employer calls unexpectedly and asks if you have time to interview right now, ask to reschedule.** You want to have everything you need in front of you and be prepared. It is okay to say that you are not in a place where you can speak openly and ask to schedule a time and date that would be convenient for them.

- **You want to be able to sit at a desk and have your resume, interview prep notes, and job descriptions close to the phone at all times.**

- **Dress the part**—put on your business suit just as you would for an in person interview.

- **Have a place already set up for the interview.** This should be a quiet room where there is a desk or table by the phone. On the desk you should have a file folder for each job you have applied to. In that file should be a copy of the job description, and your four-column list of what they are looking for, how you match that skill, and scenarios to back up your answers (covered in preparing for the interview). Your resume should be out as well, along with a pen and blank paper. Any other info about the company should be taken out of the file and placed on the desk as well in case you need to access it.

- Have your list of questions to ask the employer already prepared and at your fingertips.

- **Have your 30-second commercial out, as well as your strengths and weaknesses, and the STAR scenarios you have prepared.**

- **Put a mirror on the wall in front of you or on the desk so you can see yourself. SMILE**—people can hear a smile through the telephone.

- **If you are extremely nervous, walk around with the phone to your ear.** This will help to release some nervous energy. One of my staff members used a headset and paced around her office using this head set with a long phone cord. She said that this helped her concentrate and got her nervous energy out so that it did not come through her voice on the phone.

- **Practice an interview on the telephone with your friends and family and ask them to comment on your voice and speech qualities over the phone.** Record it and play it back for yourself. You can use a site like www.freeconference. com or your computer.

- **Be sure you keep a list of the names and titles of everyone you speak with.** You need to send a thank you to each person. If you don't want to ask a potential employer how to spell his or her name, call back and ask the receptionist for the correct spelling.

- **Before you hang up, ask about the next step in the process (see questions to ask the employer).**

The Situational Interview

This interview is very similar to the behavioral interview and is also frequently used. The interviewer will ask you to describe a situation or give an example of an event. For example: *"Describe a situation where you assumed a leadership role."* Another might be, *"Give me an example of how you motivated others to get a job done."* The STAR formula should be used here as well.

The situational interview is a little easier, because usually the trait the company is looking for is defined in the question. In the above question, the interviewer is looking for your ability to motivate others and the leadership skills you used. In the behavioral interview, the clue for competency may be hidden.

Tips for the Situational Interview

- **Do your homework.**
- **Research the company.**
- **Read and reread the job description to look for clues as to what the core competencies are.**
- **Prepare your job description tool sheets.**
- **Prepare your tool sheets of your seven stories,** and study them as they relate to the knowledge, skills, and abilities in the job description.

- **Be thorough and complete.** Remember, your goal is to show your competency through your seven stories via the STAR concept. Make sure you cover each piece and describe the situation in a way that proves your competency.

The Case Interview

If you are pursuing a career in management consulting or investment banking, you will definitely experience the case interview. However, this style and format may be used in any field. If you are interviewing for a teaching position, you may be given a case interview that involves a case/situation with a student, and you may be asked to formulate a plan, solve a problem or make a decision. If you are interviewing for a social work position, you might be given a case involving a client. No matter what position you are interviewing for or what career you are pursuing, you may encounter this type of interview. Because it is most often used in the business sense, I will illustrate as such.

In this instance, interviewers are interested in discovering how you would approach a business dilemma or challenge/situation. They are evaluating your problem-solving abilities, your thought process, your communication skills, quantitative skills, analytical skills, creativity, ability to critically think under pressure, and your ability to sell your solution via persuasive presentation skills. The interviewer will present you with a case and ask how you would handle it/solve it/advise a client. There may be no right or wrong solution. Sometimes they are looking for a correct answer. The interviewer may ask you to "think out loud" so that he or she can follow your thought process. Even if that is not the case, thinking out loud is okay.

A sample case might be: Cara's Coffees, a national chain of coffee stores, wants to expand their Northeast presence. It is their thought that the best locations are areas where there are Starbucks. They want your team's help to determine how to grow their Northeast presence. How would you help them tackle this challenge and accomplish their goal?

By now you have studied cases in school and should know the fundamentals. This is the time to apply them, not to learn them. The case interview tests your knowledge and application of that knowledge. If you need to feel more confident, go back and reread your cases from class or purchase a book written on case interviewing. However, you should be rereading for application, not to learn the fundamentals.

In a case interview, the interviewer is looking for:

- **How you think**—Is your thought process logical?

- **General business knowledge**—What relevant factors will you consider when critically thinking and problem solving and making your recommendations.

- **How much you have retained from your studies**—Do you know your formulas and theories and can you apply them? It is okay to mention them as you use them. These might be SWOT analysis, Porter's Five Forces, The Four P's of Marketing, etc.

- **Overall knowledge**—Are you making logical assumptions to recommend a solution? For example, you might reasonably guess that a single Starbucks may sell several hundred or thousands of cups of coffee every day; if you guess that they sell a million cups, there would be concern about your overall knowledge of the real world.

- **Calculations**—Interviewers won't expect you to do advanced math without the tools, but they will expect you to be able to explain how you calculate.

- **Your creativity**—Interviewers are not looking for you to come up with outlandish solutions (like burning down the Starbucks), but they will love innovative ideas that are a bit unusual or in line with current day strategies such as using social media as a marketing strategy or featuring muffins based on Cara's grandmother's old country recipes and explanations of how you came up with the thought. This is a chance to showcase your creative and critical thinking skills.

- **Communication skills**—The interviewer wants to follow your logic, so you must express your thoughts and/or decisions in a systematic way and be prepared to sell or defend your ideas. Your overall presentation will be evidence of your ability to connect with others and communicate your ideas.

- **Presentation**—Professional demeanor is important here and engagement of those who are listening.

- **Persuasive skills**—What evidence will you provide to the client to persuade them that your solution meets their needs and solves their problem. Your answer must exhibit some selling skills.

- **There are many resources that you can use to guide you in the case interview.** Check out www.wetfeet.com for information. Also, you can find some case interview information on McKinsey's website and Bain and Com-

pany as well. Check the resource page of
www.collegetocareercoaching.com

If you are committed to finding a job in management consulting, then your interview preparation should include reading the book, Case In Point, by Marc P. Cosentino and Chris Glasser. This is the best tool I have found for case interview preparation.

Brain Teaser Interviews

Another style of interview and a very challenging one. You might be asked to solve a brain-teaser type puzzle that has no relation to business at all. This interview is similar to the case interview in that the interviewer wants to understand how you think and solve problems. Just remember, your approach to the problem counts more than the solution. A typical example of a brain teaser question might be: Why are sewer covers round? An answer might be so that they can be moved easily by rolling them. If you want to build more competence in brain teaser interviews there are books written about them that you can buy at most any bookstore or see the resource page at www.collegetocareercoaching.com

Panel Interviews

The panel interview is one of the most stressful interviews. It is done by a group of people and is one of a few different types of group interviews and can be orchestrated in two ways.

In the first, there is no system or procedure, and each person on the panel asks questions that they have created around issues that are important to them. The panel is often made up of a human resources person, a line manager, your potential direct manager, that direct manager's boss, and a peer. It may also include other people that you would come in contact with in the position that you're applying for. For example, if you are applying for an entry-level accounting position in a company, the accounts payable manager may sit on the panel.

The second type of panel interview may include the same type of participants, but it is carefully orchestrated with each member of the panel having a preplanned, specific focus. For example, the human resources member might focus on your interpersonal skills and ask behavioral questions, while your direct manager may focus on your technical skills using case type questions.

Why Do Companies Choose the Panel interview?

1. **It shortens the hiring time.** Having everyone involved in the hiring decision present allows for an immediate meeting of the minds to decide if you are the best candidate. It also allows the group to set aside one day to interview many candidates. Think of it like the auditions for *American Idol*.

2. **Everyone on the panel can witness and hear your answers instead of relying on the interpretation of the single interviewer.** This allows them to discuss their thoughts and opinions together and make a decision collectively. As a recruiter, this is one of the reasons I like the panel interview.

3. **It's a learning experience for each member of the panel. Each interviewer has an expertise that the others may not.** The panel interview allows each person to learn about the other's expertise and what is important to them. While this does not really affect you, it helps the members of the panel learn what the other members look for in a candidate and helps to cover all the requirements of the position.

The panel interview may be your first interview on site at the employer, or it may be your second or final interview. Either way you need to be prepared.

Strategies to Ace the Panel Interview

- **When you enter the meeting, walk in with a confident stature and make eye contact.**

- **Introduce yourself:** *"Hello, I am Jane Smith, B.S. Marketing from The University of Miami. It is nice to meet all of you."* Initiate a firm handshake with each person and make eye contact with each.

Key Advice on eye contact: When you shake hands with a person, you only have successful eye contact when you notice the color of his or her eyes. You will see this mentioned throughout this book.

- **Take notes.** Have a professional-looking folio with you that includes a pad, pen, and copies of your resume inside. When you sit down, draw a horizontal line at the top of your paper and place the name of each panel member on the spot on the line where they sit. This will help you refer to each person by name.

- **Jot down little notes that will help you remember what was important to each member.** For example, if the direct manager asks you a question about your strengths, you can write strengths under his name. If he or she tells you that you will work in teams, you can write teams under his or her name. This will help you with your thank you note after the interview.

- **When answering a question,** begin by making eye contact with the person who asked the question, but make sure to glance at each person while you answer, and as you finish your answer, return your eye contact to the person who initiated the question.

- **Watch your body language.** This is the same for any interview. You must sit up straight and look attentive. Do not sit back or lean back in your chair. This type of posture shows a laid back, casual attitude. The best posture to have is leaning slightly forward as though you are sitting on the edge of your chair.

- **Create a list of questions to ask the panel before you go to the interview.** Have them on the second page of your pad.

- **Make sure you get each person's business card, so that you have email addresses for your thank you notes.**

- **When the interview is over,** and after you have asked the questions outlined later in this book, close with: *"Thank*

you for taking the time to meet with me, I am very interested in the position and look forward to the next step." Shake hands again with eye contact.

Key Advice: Each person gets an individual thank-you note, with different content, and the notes must be sent out before your head hits the pillow that night. Email is fine.

Calm your nerves: If you are very nervous, wiggle your toes in your shoes. Nobody can see you do it and it will draw some nervous energy away. Keep a cloth handkerchief in your right pocket for your hand shake. It can help alleviate sweaty palm before a hand shake.

The Tag Team Interview, or, The Relay Race

The tag team interview is similar to the panel interview and the group interview. However, in the tag team interview, each person is focused on a different aspect and questions you accordingly. In addition, you will be interviewed separately by each person. The tag team interview is usually a second or third interview, and takes place over the course of a day or half-day.

Each interviewer will question you on an aspect of the position, usually a technical skill set and soft skill set, and most likely, one in which the interviewer is proficient.

Think of a relay race where the person hands the baton to the next person. Only in the tag team interview, each interviewer will give a summary of his or her thoughts to the next interviewer and will offer his or her opinion on what your strengths are, and most importantly, what his or her concerns are.

The next interviewer in line will focus on his/her own area of interest and may ask questions related to the prior interviewer's concerns.

Several things will happen with this process. You will be able to tell by the questions being asked how you are doing. If the interviewer switches to topics discussed by previous interviewers, there is a concern. If the interviewer switches to a selling mode, there is a significant interest.

Tips for the tag team interview

- **The good news: you are a contender**. The company would not take the time otherwise. When this interview is scheduled, you should be told whether it will be half or full day, who you will be meeting with, and their titles. If you haven't received this info several days before the meeting, call and ask for it.

- **Google every interviewer listed**. Find out their role, time with the company, and any other public information. Enter their name in the search box on the company website, so that you find all the information listed there. Check LinkedIn, Facebook, and Twitter., and do a search with their name in quotes.

Client Story

A former client of mine was flown to Ohio to interview with a company and received his agenda one week before the meeting. It was a full day of meetings. When we Googled each person, it became clear to us that this would be a tag team interview. His first interview was with a senior human resources person. According to her profile on the company website, she had been with the company for 15 years having started as an administrative assistant and worked her way up to senior vice president.

My client was even more excited about the company, because it was obvious that there was great growth potential, and that great work was rewarded. He mentioned to her that he had read her profile and asked what knowledge, skills, and abilities it took to accomplish this feat. She was impressed with his research and her answer told him what she was looking for. This gave him the clues he needed to sell himself the rest of the day. He got the offer.

- **Prepare ahead of time.** Write important notes on the pad which is inside your portfolio about each person who you will be interviewed by, title, role, time with the company, accomplishments, and any questions you may have for them. They will be impressed with your research and preparation.

- **If questions are repeatedly being asked about the same skill or experience,** the interviewers are concerned about this area, and it is important to the position. Refocus your efforts to define your strengths in this area.

- **Often the most senior decision maker is last.** You will no doubt be tired by then. Do not be afraid to ask to use the rest room. Take a quick break and breathe.

- **It's okay to take notes in this process.** Often there will be a few minutes between interview sessions. Jot down things you might want to remember or any questions you might want to ask the next interviewer and anything you want to include in your thank you to each interviewer.

- **Ask each person what his or her role in the company is, and how you would interact with his role, department, etc.** Ask what he or she feels are the most important skills and characteristics one must have to succeed in this position with the company.

- **Get everyone's business card, and send each person a separate thank you note,** with different content, before your head hits the pillow that night. If you have to catch a flight and won't return home until very late, it is okay to email the next morning, but it is best if you do it as soon as you arrive home. You can write the notes on the plane and email them when you land. If you have your laptop with you, do it right away. The best thing about this interview is that very often, offers are made at the end of the day, or at the very least, compensation will be discussed.

The Group Interview

Similar to the panel interview, there is more than one type of group interview as well. One type of group interview involves several candidates being interviewed together. This may be done by panel or a single interviewer. Most often there are at least two people interviewing. As one questions, the other will observe. They will usually take turns asking and observing. Go back and review the tips for the panel interview, as they apply here as well.

A second type of group interview involves the candidates interacting with each other. This mode is often used by management consulting firms. In this type of group interview, a case might be given, and the group works together to prepare its answers as a group to present to the interviewer or interviewers. Alternately, each candidate may be asked to prepare his or her own answer and present it to the group, while the rest of the group is asked to respond to the candidate's presentation with questions to the candidate/presenter.

The group interview warrants some specific pointers:

- **Participate:** You must participate and ask questions in a non-challenging way. How you participate will be evaluated. If your team is presenting, make sure your attention is on the presenter and the audience. Your body language should show that you are listening with enthusiasm and simultaneously connecting with the audience. If the presenter falters come to their rescue and help out, but only after you give them time to regain their composure.

- **Take initiative:** Offer your help and thoughts. Take on tasks that utilize your strengths.

- **Listen:** How you listen to others will be observed.

- **Maintain professionalism always:** Handle yourself as if you were in a boardroom. Even though you will be working with your peers, never forget that this is an interview. Do not be casual.

- **Complete the task the interviewers have asked you to do.**

> **Client Story**
>
> My client, a Georgetown University grad, was interviewing with a management consulting firm. In the third round of interviews she was placed on one of several teams of other grads interviewing for entry-level positions. Her team was given a case and they had to work together and present it to the group and sell their solution. The job of the other candidates who were not at that moment presenting was to listen and ask questions. Each team had to present their case with the rest of the candidates listening, questioning, and probing.
>
> This was a very stressful and intense interview. My client followed the above and eventually received an offer. Her comment to me was that the most challenging part for their team was anticipating what questions they might get from the rest of the group. To prepare, they discussed what questions they might receive and formulated responses. As a result they felt more confident.

The Meal Interview

The meal interview may be breakfast, lunch, or dinner. It is usually the final interview before an offer is made and may include senior management, staff at peer level, or just your direct manger. Many meetings, no matter what industry, take place at a meal. Most often, this interview is done to observe how you handle social situations, to evaluate your interpersonal skills, and to judge your ability to maintain your professionalism in any situation. Your confidence level will be judged as well. It can be difficult to maintain your confidence level when having to eat and answer questions at the same time.

Important pointers for meal interviews

- **Take your seat only after all the interviewers have been seated**. When they stand to leave, be on your feet too.

- **Allow the interviewer to order first.** If he or she defers to you, then go ahead and order first.

- **Order food that is easy to eat.** Something you can eat with a fork or knife will allow you to eat a piece at a time. Do not order anything you have to eat with your hands or is messy.

- **Break bread into small pieces**. Remember bread on the left and drinks on the right.

- **Order something similar to your interviewer's meal.** If he or she orders a hamburger, do not order the lobster.

- **Never order the most expensive thing on the menu.**

- **Never order an alcoholic beverage, even if the interviewer does.**

- **Never be casual no matter what your interviewer says or does.** Sometimes the conversation will get casual. The interviewer may say that they were out late last night at a club or mention something personal. Don't offer up any personal information about yourself. Remember, this is still an interview, and you are being evaluated. This is an important point to remember in any interview.

- **Men, if your interviewer is a woman, remember your manners.** Open doors, let her order first, stand up when she stands up.

- **Do try to sit directly across from your direct manager, unless you are instructed differently by him/her.** If a round table, then sit as close to being directly across from him/her. If it Is just the two of you and you are seated at a table for four, then sit directly across, never next to.

The Virtual or Online Interview

Welcome to the newest technology in interviewing. This new interview is often used when the interviewer is based in a location other than where the position will be based. You may be interviewing for an IT position where your manager is based in another town or state. The virtual interview allows the employer to narrow down the number of candidates to a manageable level for the day he/she is in town to interview. It is usually one on one and may incorporate any of the above types mentioned above. You may be asked if you have video interview capability on your own computer, such as Skype or Ichat, or you may be instructed to go to an office in your city or town that provides this service.

Tips for the virtual interview

- **Treat it like any other interview**. This is the same, only virtual.

- **Make eye contact**. Look into the center of the screen and camera.

- **Dress professionally**. Wear a light color shirt such as a light blue with your suit, of course.

- **Clear the background.** The background behind you should be nondescript, like a wall without pictures and light in color.

- **If at home, do it sitting at a desk.** This will help you maintain a professional composure.

- **Body language counts.** Even though the interviewer cannot see your entire body, he/she can observe your mannerisms.

- **Smile.**

- **Since in this situation you cannot get a business card, ask for his/her email address.** If you miss the opportunity to ask, call the company and ask for the emails. If the person tells you they don't give out that information, let them know you just had an interview and need to email them thank yous.

Testing

Some companies may ask you to take a personality or skill-based test. They have the right to do this; try not to see it as invasive. Trust in the process. Don't try to anticipate the "right" answer; be yourself and answer honestly. If you have the right skills/personality for the job, it will be reflected in the test. If not, the position may not be the best fit, and the right job is out there waiting for you.

I always put "no calls" in my job board postings. If you call me I won't be happy. However, I am impressed that you got my phone number. But when you call you need to have something to say that piques my interest. If you say, "I have done a lot of research and I know that the company is doing xyz and I have had some experience with this in my most recent internship and your company is one that I have targeted as a place I believe I can contribute," I still won't be happy that you called, but I will ask you about your experience and skills and if you fit the job I will have you come in to meet with me and if you're good, then I will be happy that you called. Initiative is important.

Recruiter, global bank

4

Preparing for the Interview

Surefire mistakes? I hate it when a candidate tells me they are a people person. That is something that should come through and if that is all you can say, you haven't done your homework on knowing yourself. I hate it when you are rehearsed. Don't have textbook answers. I want to hear answers that are your answers and original answers. I may ask standard questions but I don't want to hear standard answers. I can hear it in your language that they are too textbook and not enough person.

**Human Resources Associate,
global public relations firm**

kay. Now that you've studied and learned the above, you're ready for your interview. Right?

Not so fast.

If you've done the self-assessment and prepared the tools in the *Tool Book and Action Planner*, you've learned a lot about yourself and how to present yourself in the best light. Now you have the foundation, but that's only half of the battle. Now you've got to prepare for each and every interview.

The more you know about each company, the job description, the company's services and projects, its history, latest news, accomplishments, its mission, vision, and values, the better you will be able to sell yourself as someone who is qualified for the job and can make a contribution to the company.

__Key Advice: Scrub your online presence.__ The number one thing you must do is CLEAN UP YOUR FACE-BOOK PROFILE and any other profile you have on the Internet. You must realize that __what you put online your prospective employer can see.__ That photo of you chugging margaritas in Cancun? Delete it. That racy shot you posted for your boyfriend or girlfriend? Lose it. It may be legal, but it's poison on your resume. Assume

that everyone can see what you post. If you don't want someone to see it, don't put it out there. Your Internet profiles are part of your resume. Keep them professional.

Do it NOW.

Arm Yourself With Information

Gather as much information as you can about the position and the company, from as many sources as you can. Here are some resources you can use when you have an interview scheduled:

Network. It may be a cliché by now, but it works nonetheless. Often the best way to get information is to find people who have first-hand knowledge of the company. That could mean they work there now, or have worked there in the past. It could also mean they have other associations with the company such as having done consulting work for the company or having sold products to the company. Maybe they've run charity events in partnership with this company. Anyone who's had any association with this company might turn out to be a valuable resource.

A great source is LinkedIn. Search on the company name and you will find people who work there or have worked there. You can email them (I suggest former employees) and ask for their advice and insight. However, if they don't respond, move on. If they do respond, ask them about the culture, tell them you are very interested in the company and will be interviewing. People are always willing to help when you ask for advice. In addition, look at their profiles. You may find someone who is in the same position you are interviewing for in another location or someone who had your position and has been promoted. You may also find someone who worked at the company previously. Check Facebook for a company page. See if anyone is tweeting about the company.

> **A word of caution:** You must tread lightly here. You don't want to be viewed as a stalker, hounding people who work at the company where you are interviewing. Keep your professionalism and respect your boundaries. You are still a prospective candidate.

Speak to your parents, your friends, your parent's friends, alumni, anyone you meet who might have knowledge about this company. Listen to their insights and advice.

> **But here's a caveat:** don't believe everything you hear. You do want to know about each individual's experience with that company. Remember, though, that everyone will have his or her unique take on the situation.

Client Story

Jill had spoken to several people who had positive things to say about a company she was interviewing with the following week. Then she spoke to a college acquaintance who had actually worked for the company. Her friend did not have a good experience there—she and her boss had clashing personalities, and she was terminated after only a few months. Jill was ready to cancel her interview. My advice to Jill was to realize that she shouldn't automatically assume that she would have the same type of experience her friend had encountered. The company, and the job, were perfect for Jill. I thought she should take her friend's negative experience into account but make her own judgments after the interview. Jill ended up getting hired and being very happy with the position.

Surf the Net. In many ways, the Internet can be a job seeker's best friend. There is an incredible amount of information available at the click of a mouse. Just about every company has a web presence today, and there are several ways you can tap into them:

Go to the company site. This is the first, and most obvious stop on your Internet tour. Read over every inch of the website. Click on every available option. Some sites will include more information than others, but every one will give you the inside scoop on some important aspects you should know about. Most companies have an "About Us" section. This section will often tell you about the company's history. In many cases, it will also introduce you to the company management, including bios and photographs.

Client Story

Evan, a client of mine who had an interview set up with a large financial services company, went to their website, clicked on About Us, and found a bio and photo of the manager with whom he was about to meet. The profile included the fact that she had started in the company as an account assistant, and was promoted to a senior position in PR. That gave Evan some clues to her character, and enabled him to create some questions for the interviewer. When asked if he had any questions, Evan said, *"I read in your bio that you started here as an account assistant. If I wanted to accomplish what you have, what would I need to do? What kind of characteristics would I have to have?"* This kind of question is flattering to the individual (be sure not to overdo it), and it also shows that you have done your homework. Use the site's search function to find the person you're scheduled to meet. If his or her name doesn't come up, study some of the other profiles to see if you can get a feel for the type of person who works there.

After "About Us," go to the "News" or "Press" section of the site that contains articles and public relations releases about the company. There may be information there you need to know; for instance, if the advertising agency you're considering has recently acquired a smaller firm, you don't want to be surprised when the interviewer mentions this as an important aspect of the company's growth mission.

Check out the job description section if there is one. Remember, though, that a job description is generally a wish list. An employer sits down and says, *"If I found the ideal employee, he or she would have these five qualities...."* They don't really expect that every candidate will fill all five requirements to the same extent. When I am recruiting, I always have a wish list but know what I have to have and what I can live without. Don't be concerned if you don't match all five perfectly. Instead, use them as the basis for more questions. You might say, *"According to your job description, you are looking for these five characteristics. Can you tell me how each of those attributes contributes to the job?"* You must then let the employer know how your talents and skills fit those attributes, and how you can adapt your skills to compensate for a shortcoming in the one area for which you are not a perfect match. Draw from your seven stories to **Create a Memory.**

Check The Careers Section. Often, a company will have profiles of staff in different positions. You can learn a lot about the type of person they hire from this section.

Look outside the company site for information. Check out other sites that can give you information about the company. Visit www.hoovers.com or www.Bloomberg.com for well-documented financial information.

Log onto www.wetfeet.com, which is a great site not only for company profiles, but also contains an informative section called "Careers and Industries," which lists the types of jobs (e.g., accounting) in industries and tells you about people who actually have this kind of job, what their backgrounds are, and what they do on a day-to-day basis.

Google, Google, Google. After you've checked out the company site, see what data you can obtain from other sources. Use Google, or any other search engine, to search for any tidbits that might add to your information arsenal.

You can search by:

Company name: This will give you a broader scope of news items than you will find on the company's own site, especially if there are any negatives about the company that have been in the news lately. Naturally, these probably won't show up on the company's own website. You might also find positive information that hasn't yet been posted on the company's site. Either way, you should always know the latest.

Executive's name: Search for the name of the person who's going to interview you.

Client Story

Before one of my clients interviewed with an executive at a top tier bank, we Googled the interviewer. To our surprise, we found an interview that she had done for Monster.com. She was talking about the interview process, and specifically what she looked for when hiring entry-level candidates. This was extremely useful information, as you can imagine. You may also find search results that are not job-related, such as a charity event the company held or attended, community awards they have been given, or "outside" sports activities or hobbies like a company baseball or bowling team. This kind of information can help you make a personal connection—and a memorable impression—during the interview.

Articles: Your Google search may turn up articles that are not solely about the company or particular executive, but in which either or both may have been mentioned or quoted. You can also search at www.findarticles.com, a site that archives thousands of newspaper and magazine articles.

Use the social networking sites. Go to websites like LinkedIn, to see some profiles of people who work for the company. Facebook is another good site. You may find some recent grads or alumni who now work there who you can contact.

Go to www.stumbleupon.com and search for the company name, and read what might be pertinent.

Visit www.twitter.com. People from the company may be tweeting, including the person who might be interviewing you.

The above websites may be sources of valuable information for you to prepare for the question, *"Do you have any questions for me?"*

Here's something extra: when you Google, click on "show options." Look on the left-hand side of your screen and you will see a list that says videos, blogs, forums, etc. Click on blogs and you will see blogs where the company is mentioned.

Go straight to the company. Don't forget that the company itself can be a great source of information. If they are a public company call the company's main number and ask to have their annual report sent to you. You may be able to find it on the Internet as well.

Read. What books, articles, etc. have been written about the industry in which you are interviewing? What industry specific magazines and publications have you read lately?

When I interviewed new grads, I always asked them what books they were reading.

Rule: you must always be reading to enhance your skill and knowledge.

What is being said about the company in industry publications?

What are the leaders in this industry saying?

Who are the competitors of the company you are interviewing with?

Have they done anything newsworthy?

If you are interviewing with General Electric, you should know that Jack Welch, the former CEO, has written books and is frequently interviewed. You should know that Jeff Immelt, his successor, is also frequently in the news. Find their work, read enough to know their philosophies and current thoughts, etc., before your interview.

Scout it out. Go to the place of your interview before the day of your interview and get the lay of the land. Find the street, building, etc. If it is a building with several floors, go in and check out the lobby. Knowing where you're going and arriving there before the interview, will help to calm your anxiety. In addition, as mentioned earlier, it is **never** okay to be late.

Arrive at your interview early, but no more than 15 minutes early. If you are more than 15 minutes early, wait in your car or walk around the block. When you enter, greet the receptionist, if there is one. Then sit in the waiting area and observe. Many people will be sitting in the waiting area as you are—people such as sales representatives, business executives, other candidates, etc. You can observe how people in the company interact with others. You will get a feel for the company culture, atmosphere, and the type of people who work there. You will get a vibe if the place is friendly, stiff, conservative, etc. Being there early allows you to get settled and will help reduce your anxiety.

Client Story

My client, Jonathan, was interviewing for a position at a bank. The corporate headquarters was in a large branch, which was also the waiting area for anyone visiting headquarters. He arrived there 15 minutes early to observe. He watched the branch staff interact with the bank clients. He liked what he saw and heard. The staff all appeared to be trained in a similar way. When his interviewer asked if he had any questions, he told her about his experience, and how he really liked the way the staff interacted with the bank clients. He said that it increased his desire to work there even more and asked about the training. The interviewer told him that she was impressed with his observations and questions.

Know How To Sell Yourself

A word about selling yourself. In order to sell yourself you must know what your "features" are and the "benefit" of your features. One of your features might be that you have excellent critical thinking skills. But how does this benefit the company? Critical thinking is a necessary skill for problem solving. So depending on the position you are interviewing for, the benefit might be that you have a strong ability to solve problems. Solving problems will help the company grow and generate increased profits. However, saying that you are a problem solver is not enough. You need to have an example/ story of the benefit your problem solving ability resulted in. It might sound like this: *"I have very strong critical thinking skills (feature) which helped me become an excellent problem solver. As an example, in my internship with XYZ Company, we had X problem and (example of critical thinking) as a result we were able to achieve Y..."* So you have your feature, your benefit, and the story that illustrates this along with result.

This is where the *Tool Book and Self-Assessment and Discovery* process comes in. But even if you don't have the tool book there is adequate information in this book to help you. You need to understand how your education, project work, internships, jobs, and life experiences have shaped who you are as a person and as a candidate for this position. Understanding these experiences will provide the information you need to formulate your personalized answers to questions based on your experiences and who you are. Again, seven stories.

Employers want to know the real you. They will remember your stories, in which there will be evidence of the traits and skills they are looking for. The assessment will provide you with the knowledge of your strengths and weaknesses. It will also help you define your project experiences, internship experiences, jobs, etc and help uncover your skills, knowledge, and abilities.

The tools in the tool kit will help you transfer that knowledge to action sheets, which can help you craft the answers to just about any question. If you do not have the tool book, create your own tool sheets and see the Appendices at the end of this book for examples. For each job you interview for, the tool kit and assessment can provide you with the information you need to describe how your experiences and education have given you the skills and abilities described in the job description. Most importantly, your answers will be about you. You could stand out against your competition and... *Create a Memory.*

Practice, Practice, Practice

Grab a friend or two or a group and practice your answers.

Give them a list of questions and have them interview you. Use the questions you fear most and master them. Do the same for them and critique each other.

If your career services office offers mock interview sessions, go there and practice repeatedly until you feel comfortable. Show them the job description and ask them to question you according to the skills needed. The more you practice, the more your anxiety will decrease.

Have a friend or an adult family member interview you on the phone and record it. You will hear how you sound, and listening to your responses to questions will help you refine them. Also do this with a web cam if available. You can also use a flip camera or a video camera. Remember you can secure a conference line at www.freeconference.com and practice the interview and record it. You will need a paying membership to record but it is very inexpensive.

Social Networking

Warning Again: If you have a Facebook, MySpace, or other public profile, you must remove any unprofessional pictures and information that you do not want a potential employer to see. Employers will do their research on you. They look at Facebook, MySpace, LinkedIn, Twitter, etc.

Yes, you have a legal right to post unprofessional photos or content online. And guess what? Potential employers have the right to look at your content and decide that they don't want to hire you. Are your spring break photos really worth a career?

Your profiles on social sites are now part of your resume. Use these sites to your advantage by showing and talking about your accomplishments.

Surf the other networking sites to find information about others interviewing and job search experiences. You may find people who have interesting information and/or interviewed with the company you are about to interview with.

Have all Your Facts Correct

When you arrive at your interview, you will probably be asked to fill out a paper or online application. Make sure you have your correct dates of employment, and that they match with those on your resume. Make sure your GPA is correct, and that you have the exact title of your degree. When a company decides to make you an offer, someone will usually check references or will make you an offer pending reference checks. I have seen companies rescind offers due to misinformation.

Background checks have become more common place as well as credit checks. When you fill out the application, read the paragraph or fine print, associated with the signature line. It will usually indicate that you are giving permission to check references and that may include, even though not written, credit and other personal information.

You Are Interviewing the Company

Don't forget to find out if this is a company that **you** want to work for.

Prepare the questions you want to ask before the interview. Write them down on the second page of the pad that is inside the portfolio that you are bringing. Use your company research, the job description, and your criteria to craft these questions. (see questions to ask the employer)

Know What You Are Looking For

- You have had your education, your internships, and life experiences. Now you want to get hands-on experience in the career you have chosen and build a knowledge and skill base in that career.

- How will this job opportunity provide it?

- How far do you want to travel?

- How much can you afford for commuting expenses?

- What is the company culture?

- What are the people like?

- What advancement opportunities are there?

- How long have employees in your department been with the company? If you are interviewing with an established company and many people have been in their positions for less than two years...beware, unless of course they've been promoted.

- Is employee development important to you, and how does the company feel about it?

You must know what is important to you before you go in for the interview in order to craft some questions. Your research will help you.

Key Advice: Turn off your cell phone before the interview. Make it a habit that once you enter the building you turn it off. If you forget and it rings during the interview, quickly turn it off and apologize. Never take a call during an interview and never text. In fact, do not do these things even while waiting in the waiting area.

"You can never go wrong being overdressed" is a good rule of thumb. We are a more creative industry so if anything we might be more liberal. I am not big on seeing your toe rings or your body piercings or your tattoos. When you come here you will see people dressed in jeans and wild outfits, You can do that when you work here, but right now you don't, so you need to dress, which shows me that you are taking this seriously. You need to be presentable and professional and carry yourself in a way that says, I care about this interview, I understand how to function in a work environment. There is a difference in coming here to interview and working here. If you roam our halls, people are wearing jeans and weird attire and sandals. If you are interviewing here you need to be a step above that. You need to prove yourself.

Human Resources Associate,
global public relations firm

5

Dress For Success

If a woman wears pants to my interview, I seriously will consider not hiring her. This is a very buttoned-up place. If you can't dress the part for the interview, then I think the job is not that important to you and I am concerned about how you will present every day on the job and in the senior executive meetings. Besides, when someone dresses for an interview with me, I feel respected. You can never go wrong with a skirt suit so why not just wear it instead of pants. Same for men... buttoned up, suit, tie, polished shoes.

**Former Sr. Vice President of HR,
top-tier global bank**

ou want to make an excellent first impression. When you take the time to dress professionally, the interviewer gets the impression that this interview is important to you, and that you take it seriously. He or she feels respected.

You want to look and feel confident. When you look good, you feel good. Most importantly, you want the interviewer to focus on you and not be distracted by your clothing, perfume, etc.

Plan what you will wear before the interview and try it on. Check for missing buttons, loose threads, and any spaghetti stains or spots that you might not have remembered. Make sure everything is pressed and ready to go. A suit is always the choice for men and women. Whether in the PR world or fashion world, a suit is the choice. You do not have to compromise on style when choosing a suit. Even if the company is casual, you must dress professionally for your interviews. When you are working there, you can dress like everyone else.

Key Advice: Unless you are applying for a position at a trendy boutique, stay away from clothing and accessories that have designer names or insignias. Example: No Louis Vuitton bags, or Gucci loafers, Hermes belts, Coach purses, Rolex watches, etc.

Nose rings, piercings, etc.

If you are going to wear these piercings everyday to work then I am not going to insist that you not wear them to the interview because you should be yourself. If you have a tongue piercing and can substitute a clear one or one that looks natural, I would recommend it. My concern is not that the company will discriminate. My concern is that piercings can be distracting and you want the interviewer to focus on you and not your piercings. I spoke with a campus recruiter who told me that he had interviewed a graduating senior who had a tongue piercing which he did not switch before the interview. He had found it extremely distracting and couldn't remember much of the interview other than the piercing.

Tattoos

This is similar to body jewelry. If your tattoos are always going to be visible when you work there then I would not cover them up. However, if possible, you should for a couple of reasons:

1. They could distract the interviewer. You want the interviewer to be focused and concentrating on you, not trying to figure out what your tattoo means, what it is, or what it represents.
2. Many people feel that tattoos are not professional attire and if you are interviewing in a professional environment then keep them covered.

3. Even if the company is a graphic design firm or internet marketing firm and tattoos are dress code safe, again, let's keep the recruiters attention on you.

Grooming for men and women

It's probably the most important and is step one. Your hair should be clean and well groomed. There is no excuse for not getting a hair cut if you need it. If it's been months since you have had a highlighting and you have very noticeable roots, get it done prior. Your nails and your shoes will be noticed. Personal hygiene is also key, so is fresh breath, and no cologne or perfume.

Some people are allergic to perfume and cologne. Do not take the chance that your interviewer is one of them.

Some Specifics for Men

- *A conservative suit.* Dark colors (navy or gray), preferably navy. It does not have to be expensive, but does have to fit well and be pressed.

- *Long-sleeve collared shirts,* even when it is hot. Choose white, light blue, or conservative stripes. Always wear an undershirt.

- *Tie:* Avoid bright colors, distracting patterns, theme, funky, or cartoon characters. Solid ties or stripes are best.

- *Shoes:* I can't say enough about shoes. They make the outfit. Have you ever seen someone wearing a nice suit with old beat up shoes? What did you think? Make sure your shoes are polished, and if you need a new pair, make the investment. Black is best. If you are not sure what to choose, ask the salesman.

- *Socks:* Wear dark socks that are high enough so that no skin shows when you sit down and cross your legs.

- *Jewelry:* A conservative watch is good enough—nothing else. It does not have to be expensive. Leave the expensive watch at home.

- *Belt:* wear one that matches your shoes with a simple buckle.

- *Coat:* If you wear one, it must be a conservative business overcoat. If you don't have one, buy one or borrow one. It does not have to be very expensive, and you will need one anyway once you begin your job. Black, navy, brown, or gray will do. If it is raining, wear a trench coat and carry an umbrella. Every professional man has these items, and you will need them eventually. I recommend making the investment.

- *Grooming:* Hair cut, trimmed beard, or clean shave. Nails cut and clean.

- *No cologne!* You are not going out on a date. You must not give off a noticeable scent.

- If the interview is over a meal, *carry a toothbrush in your case.* If you will be going back to the office to continue the interview use it in the restaurant bathroom before you return to the office.

- *Carry a small briefcase with a leather- or vinyl-bound folio with a pad and pen in it.* Make sure the pen writes.

Some Specifics for Women

- *Stockings:* A must! Even in 100-degree weather! Nude tones are best.

- *Carry an extra pair of stockings in your bag in case of runs.*

❦ *Jewelry:* Minimal, understated, and conservative is the rule. I recommend small pearls in your ears (you can buy costume). Leave the diamonds at home. One earring per ear is preferable. Wear only a watch, no bracelets. Nothing flashy, nothing dangling from your wrist. Choose something subtle that compliments your wrist. No rings is preferable.

❦ *Nails:* Have a manicure, and wear only clear or sheer polish. Your hands will be noticed, and the polish should not draw attention. I would not wear a French manicure unless you are in fashion, PR, or any other industry of style.

❦ *Makeup:* Neutral and conservative. No heavy eye shadow, and lightly applied mascara is great. Use neutral lip colors as well. No perfume.

Final word

When you look good, you feel confident. When you are well groomed and dressed well, it gives the message that you are serious, respect yourself, and respect the interviewer. In addition, the interviewer will know you have a professional appearance, which is important if you will be seeing clients and attending meetings

Be armed with a project you are most proud of so that when I ask what was your greatest challenge, what was a project that you are most proud of, you can point to something. That will often make them stand out. If they can say "this is the project I worked on this summer and my most favorite part was the brainstorming part and this is why I loved the brainstorming session, or my favorite part was seeing it all come together and this is how I contributed to making it come all together," I get to see them in action and if I see you in action, you've created that memory because you've brought something you've done to life and I can say, "Hey hiring manager, this is the project they've done and this is how they participated and I think they would make a good contribution to the team because they bring the following skills to the table."

**Human Resources Associate,
global public relations firm**

6

You've Had Your Interview —Now What?

Networking is the key to getting an opportunity. As much as you can, network through contacts in the company. If an internal employee refers you as someone they know and they think you would be a great fit for us in the marketing department, etc., that's a resume I am going to take a look at. Network through friends, neighbors, a colleague, etc. Use the Internet. Linkedin—there's probably someone in your network who has come in contact with the company.

Director of Global Talent Engagement, privately held firm, financial services industry

After The First Interview

After your first interview, and all interviews, make sure to email a thank-you note to all the people who met with you. Thank them for meeting with you and reiterate your interest in the position and why you feel you are a great fit. Let them know you are looking forward to the next step.

This is also a great time to address anything that you want them to know about you that you didn't have an opportunity to say, or address any concerns that you feel the employer might have.

The Second Interview

The first interview will determine if you are a possible fit for the position. The human resources person or interview group will assess whether you have the knowledge, skills, abilities, and personal characteristics to meet the requirements of the position. If this is the case, then most often you will be invited back for a second interview probably with your future manager.

Note: *Sometimes the second interview takes place the same day as the first interview. The human resources person may have you meet with your potential manager immediately following the meeting with the human resources person. This is technically a second interview,* *but don't get discouraged if you meet only the HR person. Many times, there is a first round and then second round, sometimes even a third. When invited back for a second or third interview, make sure to ask whom you will be meeting with and their titles. "Thank you for inviting me back. Would you please tell me who I will be meeting with and their title?" If there are more than two people you are meeting with, ask if you will be receiving an agenda. This will be common for interviews that take one-half or an entire day. You will usually receive it in an email, and it will inform you who you are meeting with, when and whether, you will be having lunch, dinner, etc. Don't worry, if this is going to be a half day or full day interview it is usually well orchestrated and you will be told what to expect. However, if you are meeting more than one person in your second interview, it helps to prepare if you ask when you are being scheduled.*

The second interview will be more in-depth.

Be prepared to review your resume again with the manager. You may also be asked some of the same questions as during the first interview. Be consistent with your answers.

The manager will know more about the job and, of course, have experience in the responsibilities of the position. You will no doubt field more questions relating to your knowledge and skills. The manager will also probe to see if you are compatible with the other people in the department.

Listen carefully to the questions and look for a pattern. They will give you a hint of what the manager is probing for. Most likely it will relate to the job description.

You may be invited to lunch or to meet others in the department. These are all positive signs.

You may be asked salary and compensation questions here. Have your questions to ask the interviewer written out in advance on the pad inside your folio.

At the end of the interview, you may meet with the HR person again. If you haven't been asked about salary yet, you most likely will here. This is a sign that you are being considered. You may be asked about availability to start as well. (See question and answers in the next chapter.)

After The Second Interview

As in the first interview, send a separate email to everyone that interviewed you. Reiterate your interest, refer to your conversation, address any issues, or add anything you didn't get to say that you feel is important for them to know. It is okay to reiterate why you feel you are a great fit as well. Let them know that you are looking forward to the next step. If you follow my advice in the Questions to Ask Employers section, you will know what the next step is and when it will happen.

Special Note: *If there was an administrative person that assisted you or guided you through the day, then you must email him or her a thank you as well.*

The Third Interview

This is usually the final interview, and as mentioned above, if you follow my advice in the Questions to Ask..., you will know what this interview will be about. Often, the third interview is to meet senior management of the department or area you will work in. I call it the blessing interview, as many times, senior management must "sign off" on the hire. You may very well receive the offer in person at this interview, so you must be prepared.

When you have 100 resumes to go through, how do you pare them down?

- Easy to read.
- A recent college grad doesn't have that much to say.
- GPA is most important, if there is no GPA, I don't read it.
- A very bad GPA is below a 2.8. I don't look at it if it is under 3.0.
- If it is not there, I assume it's horrific.
- Not having gaps in work history is important. If you have a gap in the summer, I think you just took off and did nothing.
- Corporate internships usually trump non-corporate internships.
- Some grads will leave off a job because they think it's meaningless or not professional enough. For instance, a waitress—but you can get a lot of great experience being a waitress.
- Client service skills and interpersonal skills are a key thing at our company.
- Don't give me high school jobs, I want to see recent jobs.
- Activities are important to me, especially if you have had leadership roles, so if two people have the same GPA and one has activities and the other doesn't, I will meet the one with the activities.

**Human Resources Officer,
Big Four accounting firm**

7

Questions to Ask the Interviewer

What creates a memory for you and has you say, "Yes"?

Someone who has confidence and answers articulately. Someone who describes the situation, task, action, result. Tell me "this was the part that I did." I don't want to hear "we," I want to know about you. Being themselves, not a robot. I don't want a cookie cutter.

**Human Resources Officer,
Big Four accounting firm**

"What questions do you have for me?"

This is a question you can count on getting in every interview —1st, 2nd, 3rd, 14th! My clients always feel uncomfortable with this and say they don't know what to ask. Try to think of this as another way to connect with the interviewer and further your conversation.

Remember you are also interviewing to see if this company is a fit for you!

There are three categories of questions:

1. Questions you craft before the interview.
2. Questions that will occur to you during your interview based on what you hear.
3. Questions you must ask in every interview.

In addition, the questions you ask should depend on who is interviewing you. There are questions for HR, the hiring manager, a potential co-worker, and the senior manager.

Number 1 and number 3 can be prepared ahead of time. Number 2 questions you will craft as you go along in the interview process.

If you have prepared the way I have laid out for you in the previous chapters, then you should be ready for this.

The Most Important Thing to Know About Asking Questions

This is a tip that you will use throughout your career and life. If you learn nothing else from this book, you must learn and practice this! Ask open-ended questions. What are open-ended questions? This is best explained by what a closed-ended question is. Closed-ended questions elicit only a "Yes" or "No" response. Open-ended questions elicit stories and you want to hear the stories. Open-ended questions will often start with "How" and "What."

For example: Let's say you want to know about employee development/growth. This is usually some form of internal training and these days many firms have internal universities and established programs for the growth/learning/development of staff.

If you ask: *"Does the company have an employee development program?"* You will get a yes or no. If no other thoughts are offered by the interviewer, you will need to ask more. However, if you ask instead: *"What is the company's philosophy about employee development?"* you will get a story. You learn much more from stories. Remember that's why the interviewer asks you open-ended questions.

Ask open-ended questions. Writing them out prior to your interview and having them at your fingertips will help you with this.

Another reason you want open-ended questions is that you want to connect with the interviewer. Now you have already been connecting with the interviewer but they have been in the authority role asking the questions. Now it's your turn to ask and their turn to answer. Although you never want to come off with an attitude, this part of the interview allows you to be in more of a shared conversation. Open-ended, well-thought-out questions with a purpose will help. This is also an opportunity to ask about the interviewer's experience, how long they have been with the company, or what projects they have been involved with.

SOME GENERIC TIPS FIRST:

- ❧ Your questions should be real questions based on what you have read in your research and heard in your interview.
- ❧ There should always be a purpose of your question.
- ❧ Your questions should be thoughtful.
- ❧ Reference how you came up with your question, such as:

"In reading the job description, it mentioned, strong written communication skills. We have not spoken about that so far, can you tell me more about that?"

(This nice open-ended question shows you did your homework and is based on your interview so far.)

Questions You Craft Before the Interview

As you do your research, jot down questions you might have about:

- The company
- The job description
- Any news/press release items you read about.
- Product lines
- Mission
- Recent mergers/acquisitions
- Employee development
- Advancement/growth potential

Examples:

"I read about your recent acquisition of XYZ Company. How has this job/role been impacted by the new products added to the company?"

"In my research, I came across an article that spoke about the company as an industry leader.

What in your opinion has led to that, and how do you maintain your competitive edge?"

"The job description notes team initiatives. I have had a lot of experience working in teams; can you tell me more about that and perhaps give me an example?"

If there is travel, you can ask about locations and logistics, etc.

You should include questions also that will help you decide if you want this job and if you want to work for this company. This is why it is important to know what is important to you. Remember, you are there to also learn more so that you can decide if this is a place you want to be.

So look at your criteria as well. For example, if growth and development is important to you (and let's face it, it should be), you might want to ask: *"I would be interested to learn about the company's thoughts on employee development and growth."*

Questions You Craft During the Interview

These are a little trickier because if you are nervous you may forget to write them down or be listening so intensely that you don't think about questions to ask. If you hear something that you want to know more about, say so. Relate it to something you have done and then ask the interviewer to elaborate. Make sure you ask questions around areas of strengths not weakness.

Examples:

"You mentioned that the person in this position will attend quarterly management meetings. Could you tell me more about that?"

"You mentioned that the position requires a lot of multitasking, I have had to do that in every one of my internships. Can you tell me more about multitasking in this position?

"When I spoke with Jennifer, she mentioned that being a team player is an important key to being successful in this position. I worked in teams in both of my internships and I really enjoy that, can you tell me more about the teamwork this position is involved in?"

Questions You Must Always Ask at the End of the Interview
At first, these might seem or feel too assertive to you, but they are necessary.

"How does my background fit with what you are looking for?"

This question is so important because it will allow the interviewer to tell you if you are an on target candidate in knowledge, skills, and abilities. It also gives them the opportunity to tell you what is missing.

"What, if anything is missing from my background?"

If they didn't answer it in # 1, this will allow the interviewer to let you know what was missing for them and it will give you a chance to tell them that you have it and give an example (remember your seven stories). Think about how hard it must be for the interviewer to learn everything they need to know about a candidate in one hour or less.

Another way to ask this is: *"Was there anything were you hoping to see in my background but didn't?"*

> **Client Story**
> When I was invited to do a workshop about interviewing at a local college, I wanted to do something different. I had been there before and wanted to change it up a little, so we did what I called "Speed Interviewing." I took two job postings off the job boards and broke the group into groups of two people each. One would be the interviewer and one would be the candidate. I met with

the interviewers and handed them the job descriptions with the soft skills (team player, organized, interpersonal skills, etc) circled. I told them their mission was to ask questions of the candidate to find out how they met the requirements of the soft skills. They had 15 minutes to interview on this. Then they switched and the former candidates got different job postings and had to do the same.

The result? It was unanimous: everyone said it was much harder to be the interviewer! They were surprised and understood how difficult it is to ascertain someone's skills in a short period of time. They thought it would still be difficult if they had an hour!

"Where do I fit within the candidates being considered for the position?"

Okay, I know you're thinking: too scary, but wouldn't you like to know where you stand with the competition? Everyone has the tendency to fall in love with a job, think they rocked the interview, and as a result, go home and wait instead of forging ahead with their job search aggressively. As a recruiter, I can tell you that sometimes there are many great candidates and if you are one of five who are great, that puts you at a 20%

chance of getting the job. This is a bold question and I always thought highly of the candidates who were not afraid to ask it. I would always tell them the truth. I might say, "We have two other candidates that we are considering, the other two have... or the top candidate has more..." This will allow you to reiterate your qualifications and interest as well as anything you left out.

"What is the next step?"

Reiterate your interest. *"I am very interested in the position and the company. Now that I have learned more about the responsibilities and qualifications, I believe my education, internships and experiences that we spoke about will allow me to excel in the position and contribute, what is the next step?"*

Questions You Should NEVER Ask in a First Interview
- How much vacation time is there?
- What are the benefits?
- What are the hours?
- What is the salary?
- When is the first performance review?

Here are some generic questions that you can review to help you craft your questions prior to the interview:

Questions for Human Resources or the first person who interviews you:

- What characteristics do you look for in a person that makes them successful here?
- Can you tell me more about the culture?
- What is it, in your opinion, that has people want to stay with the company?
- What is the company's philosophy on employee development and training?

Questions for direct supervisor (your immediate boss):

- What characteristics do you look for that make a person successful here?
- What, in your opinion, are the greatest challenges of the position?
- How does this position interact with others in this department?
- How does this position interact with other departments of the company?
- How will my performance be evaluated?
- What has been the growth path for others who have been in this position?
- Can you describe the culture and environment in this area?
- What is a typical day like in this position?

Questions for colleague in your department:
Remember, in this meeting, they are trying to ascertain if you will fit in with the others in your department. You want to connect with this person on a professional level.

- Can you describe a typical week in this position?
- How long have you been with the firm?
- What are the aspects of the position that you enjoy?
- What are the challenges of the position?
- What could you share about what it takes to be a success here?

Key advice: *Remain professional at all times in this meeting. Sometimes a colleague will get personal or overly friendly. Do not switch out of your interview mode. You can relax a little but remember, you are in an interview and this colleague is going to be asked their opinion of you by the interview team.*

Questions for a colleague in another department:
- How does this position interact with your area?
- In your opinion, what is most important about that? (Relates to above.)
- What has been your experience here?
- In your opinion, what does it take to be successful here?

Questions for a senior manager:
This is the most senior person you will probably interview with.
This is where you can use your research about the company.

- In your opinion, what characteristics make a person successful here?
- What challenges is the company facing at present?
- I read in the press release section of the website, that the company has just entered the (**what you've read**) market, how will that impact the area that this position is in?

The above question should make sense based on the position you are interviewing for. For example, if you are interviewing for an account manager position for the U.S. operations, then asking about entering the Indonesian market would not be appropriate. However, asking about a new product line just launched in the U.S. would.

Personality is important to us. What I want to see is enthusiasm. Always look someone in the eye when you are talking to them. If you cannot engage me and have a conversation you are not a good fit here. I need outgoing, assertive. I need people who can build relationships.

If you are going into PR and you have no enthusiasm, no passion, you aren't going anywhere. I cannot pass you on to the manager. If you have no energy I cannot hire you. We are client relationship builders, we are client builders, we work in teams, and you have to be able to get along with the other people. If you have no energy and can't get along with the other people, I can't hire you, forget it.

Human Resources Associate,
global public relations firm

8

Tell Me About Yourself

Advice to candidates?

Practice and prepare. Don't underestimate the work you have done. I love waitressing as experience, but if you don't think it was valuable, why would I? If all you did in your internship was get coffee and filing, then I want to know what you learned from it. Everyone likes their coffee different and if the files aren't done right people can't find things. There is importance to every task. I want to know that you understand that. Have good telephone skills.

Human Resources Officer,
Big Four accounting firm

Tell me about yourself.
What are your strengths?
What is your weakness?
Where do you want to be in five years?
What makes you the best candidate?
Where else are you interviewing?
Why do you want to work for our company?
Sell me this pen.

Most people are petrified of these questions. My clients often tell me they don't feel confident or don't know what to say. The tool book and action planner, which includes the assessment, will help you gain the insight you need to personalize your answers. But here are some tips.

Tell me about yourself.
This is your 30-second commercial. It should cover the following:

- Who you are.
- What you have done.
- Your strengths.
- What are you looking for.

Here is the secret. Know what the client is looking for and highlight that in your commercial. Make an action sheet for each job you are interviewing for and then put your commercial together (see appendix for 30 Second Commercial Action Tool.) Prepare this in advance and practice it 100 times in the mirror until you can say it naturally without being rehearsed. It doesn't matter if you don't say it exactly; if you do what I suggest, you will get most of it. Knowing that you have this done before your interview could alleviate much of your anxiety.

What are your strengths?

Do not use the typical answers—hard worker, good people person. Study your experiences and pull your real strengths from those experiences.

Always have examples to back up your statements. I always ask candidates how they know they have those strengths. So if you tell me you are resourceful, I might ask, *"How do you know that about yourself?"*

Have a minimum of five strengths to discuss, and of course choose ones that match the job description.

Examples of strengths that I like to hear: resourceful, sense of urgency, critical thinking skills, multitasker, skilled listener.

What is your weakness?

Again, the most important thing about this question is that you know what your weakness is and you take steps to correct it when it creeps up on you.

Where do you want to be in five years?

This is a question that worries all of my clients. After all, how can you know exactly what you will want to be doing in five years? Some of you might, if you're going to medical school, or want to get your masters in teaching. Then it's easy.

But what about the communications major or sociology major?

As a recruiter, I often ask this question, but in a different way. I might ask you *"What are your short-term and long-term goals for yourself?"* Either way, in my opinion, the best way to answer this question is to say that in the short term, gaining experience and contributing value to a company is your goal. As far as long term, you are not sure what path your first experience will lead you on, but along the way your goal is to gain knowledge and experience that will develop you to become a leader and respected in your field. The tool book has more on this.

What makes you the best candidate?

This is where you get to highlight your knowledge, skill, and experience as it relates directly to their job. That's exactly what you should do in this instant. Be specific—remember your stories. Prepare this answer prior to the interview and then add anything more that you gain from the interview experience.

Where else are you interviewing?

Companies expect that you are interviewing elsewhere. It's okay to answer this question.

If you are interviewing with their competitor it is okay to say *"I am in the process with two other firms in this industry, however, your company is my first choice because..."*

If you are not interviewing anywhere else at the moment, but have resumes out (and you should) it is okay to say you are in the process as above. *"I am actively in the job search process and I am pursuing companies in the X industry and the Y industry, however, your company is my first choice because..."* The "because" should be what you like about the company and also why you feel you are a good fit.

Why do you want to work for our company?

If you don't have persuasive reasons why you want to work for their company, then you need to get several before you show up for the interview. This is where your research comes in, so have something to say about the mission, the employee development, the recent news, etc.

Sell me this pen.

This question could throw anyone off if you don't know the fundamentals of selling.

To answer this question, you utilize the same concept that I discussed at the beginning of this book. Interviewing is selling yourself into the needs of the company.

So how can you sell a pen to someone if you don't know what qualities they look for in a pen?

So the way to handle this question is to ask the person what qualities are important to them in a pen. Then you can sell them the pen based on those qualities.

Example: Tell me, what qualities do you look for in a pen?

Interviewer: Well, it has to feel good in my hand, write smoothly, and have a fairly light weight.

You: What about price?

Interviewer: Something reasonable, around $5.00

You: Great, so I would like to show you this pen, which I believe meets your criteria. Please hold it and see how it feels. Write with it. How does that feel?

Interviewer: It feels good

You: Great, and it's $4.25 which is less than your top price, would you like it?

You must close the deal here.

Now the interviewer knows that you know the fundamentals of a consultative sell. You have just engaged the interviewer. Good job!

Client Story

When coaching one-on-one with my clients, we always take time to pinpoint a weakness for the *"What are your weaknesses"* question and formulate the answer. The self-assessment is key here.

After a great deal of discussion about my client's experiences and examination of her seven stories, we discovered that her weakness was that she was quick to make decisions—sometimes too quick. She had a story, of course, to depict this. What she has learned, however, is that when she is making an important decision, she does not act on it immediately. She forces herself to get feedback from others who have a stake in the outcome and then sleeps on it. As a result, she makes a much better decision.

Sample Interview Questions

At the back of this book you will find an Appendix with a list of sample interview questions. They will provide good practice for you. Remember the STAR.

Favorite interview questions?

We use behavioral interview questions. I don't ask the "Tell me about yourself" or "Strengths and weakness" questions. I feel I learn more about the person from behavioral questions such as:

- Tell me about a team project that you had that didn't progress and why. Tell me what was your role in the project; tell me about what happened.
- Tell me about the most difficult person you had to work with and how you handled it.
- How do you work with your peers?

Sometimes I get a candidate who is extremely qualified, maybe a triple major 3.8 and very confident. So I might ask:

- Tell me about a time when things didn't go well or you were disappointed in your performance.

If a candidate is very verbal and outgoing, I might ask:

- When did you have to work with someone who was quiet and shy?

Favorite interview questions?—continued

This gives me insight to leadership skills and their ability to work with people who are different than themselves.

- Walk me through a week of your life.
- Tell me about your most technically challenging class.

I don't ask what they want to be doing in five years. At such a young age, how can they know? And of course a very important question is:

- Why do you want to work for our company?

**Human Resources Officer,
Big Four accounting firm**

9

How to Overcome Rejection

I'm looking for someone who can communicate well, who listens to the questions I am asking and answers them thoroughly. I am looking for people who take ownership of their career and know the aspects of the job.

An interview is a sales job where you have to sell yourself.

GPA is important but work experience is more important.

**Controller,
law practice industry**

You Rocked the Interview... But You Didn't Get The Job

Okay, so you did everything we discussed in this book and then some. You researched, you practiced, you knew your stories inside and out. You knew your strengths and weaknesses and you answered every question with STAR and even felt the interviewer genuinely liked you. You thought it went great and you expected to be called back or get an offer but you just got an email from HR letting you know you didn't get the job. Ugh! So much work, so much time, you wanted this, you liked the company. You're thinking... what's wrong with me, I'll never get a job, I hate this, I don't think I can do this anymore, maybe I can just move home and be a kid again.

Take ten seconds to feel sorry for yourself.

Your ten seconds are up. Now it's time to get to work!

First, reexamine your interview experience. You should do this immediately following the interview when it's freshest in your mind.

- Write down all of the questions you were asked.
- Write down next to each question, the story/example you used to answer.
- Pull out the job description again and review it.

- Write down where you did well and where you feel you could have done a better and how you could have done better.
- Write down each person you met with and how you felt about your connection with them.
- If you got the interview through a recruiter ask for honest feedback.
- Move on and keep searching and keep interviewing.

Example: *Team experience—could have done better, I should have mentioned...*

You will pull this out as part of your preparation for the next interview that you go on and study it.

Practice makes perfect. Examine your experience, learn and adjust.

Sometimes, however, you've done everything right, but you just don't get the job.

Client Story

When I was recruiting for a top-tier bank in New York City, one day I received an interoffice envelope from the recruiter who was recruiting for the management training program for the bank. This was a very competitive program where new employees rotated through different areas of the bank every six months in a different country and were on a track to become senior management. I opened the envelope to find about 50 resumes and I was shocked. They were MBAs from Harvard and Yale and other top schools, had 4.0 GPAs and excellent internships, and more. I called the recruiter and asked why she sent them to me. She said they were the ones she did not hire and perhaps I had spots for them. She said she wished she could hire them all but she only had six slots.

Here's what could be really going on. There is nothing wrong with you or your experience.

There just may have been a candidate that had more experience, or was a referral from someone inside the company, or had industry experience. There could be a million reasons from practical to ridiculous.

It's very competitive out there and there is always an element of randomness. So the moral is, *maybe it wasn't you.*

Here's what you need to remember. If you have done all of the preparation in this book right down to each and every one of your seven stories, in the interview you will come across in a way that will get you the job that you are supposed to have. I know that after reading this sentence you are thinking I am crazy, but I assure you this is true. If you did not get this job, I promise you that the job you are supposed to have is out there. You want to work where you fit and can make a contribution. If you do the work I have laid out for you, this is what could happen!

My Story: From Small Beginnings Came Good Things

I would like to share with you my story. I graduated college with a Bachelor of Science in Accounting. I had a pretty good GPA but not the 3.7 required in those days to be accepted for the on-campus interviews from the biggest CPA firms. There were several women in my class who met that criteria and all got offers from these firms. Others around me kept getting offers from companies, but not me. I was so discouraged and down, but never lost my determination.

One day I saw an ad in the local newspaper for an accountant. It was a very small ad, which of course had me thinking that this was not a very special company, but I answered it anyway. I got a call for an interview and went. It was for a national temporary agency and I would be one of four accountants in the accounting department reporting to the controller. The controller was a woman and my interview went well. However, this company was a far cry from the global CPA firms I wanted to work with. I got a call the next day with an offer and when I heard the dollars, I was depressed. The controller told me that they always started out low but gave a three-month review with a decent increase. I just wanted to work—so I accepted the job.

Three months later I got a 30% increase in salary. That's right—30%! In addition, it was this job that would give me the foundation and springboard me into a very successful career in the staffing industry. It was at this company that I learned the infrastructure of the staffing industry.

Two years later, after moving back to New York, I got a call from the president of Accountants On Call (now Ajilon Finance), who asked me if I would be interested in a position with his company as a recruiter. He felt that my accounting experience in the temporary agency was a great fit for the job and he wanted to speak with me about it. Well, three years later, five years after college, I made my first six-figure income and was in a business that I would love forever and stay a part of for a very long time. That business would be a learning ground for knowledge and experience that many people don't have the opportunity to get in a lifetime. Here, I would play a key leadership role in the growth of this company from one small office into an international firm.

Moral of the story: If you do the work I have spelled out for you, you will get the job you were supposed to have.

Rejection hurts, no doubt. Reframe it. Maybe, just maybe there is something better out there for you and a place where you belong.

What are surefire mistakes that make you pass on a candidate?

Don't tell me you want to go to law school if you are interviewing for an accounting position. If your not sure what you want, how can I be?

The biggest thing is communication. If you can't articulate what's in your mind then you can't make it here. I am assessing your verbal skills in the interview.

It's amazing how many students do not know the basics of an interview. I try to make them feel comfortable and my goal is to have every student walk out feeling they did great. I try to make everyone feel comfortable. Nervous and unprepared is not good. Some nervousness is understandable but when it affects their ability to answer questions it is a problem. How can you go into a meeting with a controller or senior manager if you're intimidated by me?

**Human Resources Associate,
global public relations firm**

10

What Salary Are You Looking For?
And Negotiating the Offer

Favorite interview questions?

- Describe the ideal job you would like to have. I ask this so I can get a feel for what they like to do.
- Are you more analytical, social, etc.?
- Describe some of the projects that you have had.
- What makes you stand out?

I ask open-ended questions

**Controller,
law practice industry**

ongratulations! You have a job offer! Now what?

You may get an offer on the second or third interview. I have rarely seen it after the first interview, but it is always good to be prepared. In any event, the salary question will come up first, sometimes in the first interview, so you need to be prepared for the question:

"What salary are you looking for?"

I have a very definite opinion on this subject. As a new grad or college student, your main focus should be on the **opportunity**. You want a position that will provide the opportunity to learn, develop skills, gain experience, and make a contribution.

Salary should not be your number one priority.

Client Story

David had two offers from two very different companies. One was a Fortune 500 and the other a small company. The Fortune 500 had all the benefits, an in-house employee development program and was offering $3,000 more than the small company. The small company had decent benefits and no in-house employee development plan, although they did have tuition reimbursement. They did offer bonuses, however, which were in stock options. The company was hoping to go public in the next two years. When David came to me to discuss the two positions, we examined them in great detail. We looked at:

How did he feel when he was there? Did he like the culture, his manager, co-workers?

What would the responsibilities of the position be?

Was he passionate about the company's product or service?

What was the career path?

What happened to the previous person in the position?

What skills would he need to excel in the position?

What new skills would he learn?

Could the skills he would learn help him attain his short- and long-range goals and make him more marketable in the future?

When we looked at these questions and matched them up with David's short- and long-range goals, the small company at less money was what he chose. So far he is very happy.

But how do **you** answer the question, *"What salary are you looking for?"*

Do not blurt out a number. If it is too high, you may lose out on a great opportunity. If it's too low, you've undersold yourself. In addition, there is a difference between salary and compensation. Salary is the amount you will be paid weekly, biweekly, or monthly, and the time frame is always fixed by the company. Compensation includes, salary, any commission, and any bonus. Part of compensation are benefits which may include, health insurance, life, insurance, 401k plans, medical savings plans, etc. In addition there are performance reviews sometimes after the first six months (most often after one year), that often result in salary increases. However, you never ask about any of this prior to getting an offer. The interviewer will bring it up and then you can have the discussion.

So back to how you answer the question:
Remember, opportunity is the number one priority so here's what I would suggest. Here are two options:

1. "While salary is important to me, the opportunity is my first priority. From what I have learned so far the position presents the type of opportunity I am looking for. What is the salary range you are offering?"

2. "While salary is important to me, the opportunity to learn, develop my skills further, and gain experience is my priority. What is the salary range designated for this position?"

You want to know the range.

Be honest. Be yourself. Remember:
Opportunity #1, Salary #2.

So what if the hiring manager says, *"The range is $35,000 to $40,000, how does that sound?"*

What do you do now?

Well that's the salary but what's the compensation, remember compensation includes salary and benefits.

So first of all if the range is good, say so. If you were looking for 40k, then you could say, *"It sounds on target, however, I was hoping to be closer to the 40k, but I am at a little bit of a disadvantage because I do not know the rest of the compensation, such as contributions for health insurance, any potential year end bonuses, performance reviews, 401k, tuition, etc. Would you be able to share that with me?"*

If you are having the conversation above you are probably in your second or third interview.

Remember, this is your first career position out of college. A $2,000 difference is about $1.00 per hour. Don't pass a great opportunity by because of the money, unless of course the money is ridiculously low and you couldn't even live on it. It's important also to research salaries in your industry of choice so that you some knowledge. Use the web. Some industries pay lower than others. For example, the advertising industry and public relations are know to pay less than accounting.

What if the salary offer is not what you were hoping for?
If they told you the range was 35-40 and they offer 35, now what?

First, always say, *"thank you."* You can say, *"Thank you very much for your offer, I am very interested in the company and the position. I was hoping to be closer to the 40k, is there a little flexibility?"* This is a closed ended question and is used here on purpose because you want to know yes or no. Be prepared for *"Well, it might be, what would make you happy?"* Your answer should be , *"as close to 40k as possible."*

If the answer is "no," make sure you know the entire compensation package. You can say: *"So that I can make an informed*

decision, is it possible to get all of the information about benefits, possible bonus, performance reviews etc.?" Any company worth working for will have this info available for you and will most likely put it in writing in an offer letter. If there is flexibility in the offer, they will probably come back with 37K.

If the offer was what you were looking for, you still want to know what the rest of the compensation is. Say, *"Thank you, I am very excited about the opportunity, how can I learn more about the benefits, etc so that I can make an informed decision?"*

I know these are scary questions, but remember, once you accept the position there is no turning back. Unless there is a six-month performance review, you will be at this compensation level for the next year of your life.

You should always ask for an offer in writing. It will usually be emailed to you and you can let them know that you will read it over and call them the next day.

If you are at this point—Congratulations, you did it!!

If you don't have a network and don't have experience in networking, the nicest way to get my attention is to find someone in the firm that you can connect with and get a referral. If someone in the company calls me and says they have a referral, I always take a look at it. At the end of the day if you want to get my attention, you just have to bug me. It annoys the living daylights out of me but that's how you're going to do it.

That means you call our receptionist and ask for Human Resources and you usually get to me.

That means if I don't call you back right away then you call again and I have found great people that way. I have said, my god this person has called me six times, but still called them back and they were great. I was annoyed at being called so much but when I called them back, they were great and I think, wow, I am so glad they pestered me.

I cannot stand when people get a hold of my email address, but if you get my email address and you put yourself in front of me then I will take a look.

**Human Resources Associate,
global public relations firm**

11

The Value of a Coach

How do you know a candidate is prepared for your interview?

It's usually obvious. They have thorough and complete answers for me. Don't memorize your answers, just have it in your head. It should be easy because the interviewer is asking you about you.

**Human Resources Officer,
Big Four accounting firm**

Olympic Gold Medalist Michael Phelps
Basketball Superstar Michael Jordan
Quarterback Eli Manning
Yankee Captain Derek Jeter
The 1980 USA Olympic Gold Medal Hockey Team

What do they have in common?

Outstanding coaching... coaches who educated these champions on the rules of the game, guided them on the best way to play it, helped them to identify and capitalize on their strengths, and challenged them to maximize their potential and achieve record breaking results-results that some thought to be impossible!

My kind of coaching is no different. Working one-on-one with a coach provides you with an interactive and collaborative method of working through your self-assessment, job search strategy, and interview game plan. A coach doesn't tell you what to do or try to push you in any particular direction. Instead, you and I will work through each detail of your self-assessment.

Together we will collaborate to:
- Define your own personal strengths.
- Identify industries and companies to target.

- Explore the best way to brand and market "you."
- Educate you on the type of interviews you will encounter.
- Prepare you to finesse even the most difficult interviews with greater confidence.
- Strategize and implement your job search.
- Challenge you to achieve your goals.

Job hunting can be an overwhelming experience. Having a coach who is an expert and has "been there, done that" listen to your ideas and give you feedback makes the process faster, less overwhelming and less fearsome.

A coach helps you break down the process into well-defined steps with tasks to accomplish and goals to achieve, with checkpoints along the way.

It is not possible for me to work with everyone, so I wrote this book and developed the *Tool Book and Action Planner* to be the next best thing to working one-on-one with you. Although this tool book and action planner do not take the place of an individual coach, they will help you be your own coach.

The Tool Book and Action Planner includes examples from former clients that will serve as a guideline for you. You will learn from their stories and their completed worksheets and utilize their examples to help understand your experiences, complete your action tools, and craft your interview answers.

Every interview situation is unique. If you do the work laid out here, you could build the knowledge, skills, and ability to handle the interviewing process with confidence and ease and most importantly...

Create a Memory.

At this point, some of you will have already purchased the *Tool Book and Action Planner,* and some of you have decided to only purchase this book, Part I. In either case, the book that you are reading now is Part I, because it provides the information necessary for anyone about to begin the job search process.

SPECIAL NOTE ABOUT CAREER SERVICES

Whether I am doing an on-campus workshop, speaking to a large group, or working one-on-one with a student or new grad, I always research what the Career Services office at their school has to offer.

The Career Services office at your school can be very helpful. In recent years, they have added many tools for students in the job search process. Although they do not have the resources to give each student many hours of individual coaching as my program does, many offer mock interviews and will help you with your resume. Therefore, your campus Career Services office is a great place to begin. In addition, the Career Services office most often organizes career fairs, on-campus information sessions for corporations, and on-campus interviews. They will know the schedule of events and the requirements to participate in those events. Requirements could be that you have a particular major or maintain a certain grade point average.

Key Advice: Get to know your career services representatives. They are there to help you, and although they may not be able to provide you with hours and hours of individual coaching, they can be of great help to you and give you a head start that can only help you in my program.

New grads are always nervous about the question: "What is your weakness?"

I always ask this question and I ask it for two reasons. First, I want to hire you for what you are good at and I never want to expect you to excel where you are weak or accomplish something that you are not good at. Me expecting you to do well at something you are not good at is the definition of insanity! I want to hire you for what you are good at and then expect you to excel in that area. This makes you and me very happy, and a happy staff likes to come to work everyday. Second, I want to know that you know what you are weak at, and that you can take steps to correct it or catch it when it's happening. When a candidate has this insight and can verbalize it, it shows emotional intelligence and maturity. That's something I look for.

**Senior Vice President,
national staffing firm**

Final Note

ow that you have finished reading, you are probably thinking…Ugh! This is a lot of work.

THIS IS NOT WORK. THIS IS INVESTMENT!

Investment in yourself, your career, and your life. If you invest others will too. Right now, finding a job **is** your job.

The information in this book is designed to arm you with enough information to prepare for your interviews. It is competitive out there and you need to be prepared.

If you make the effort to prepare you will be ahead of the game and should find yourself more relaxed in the interview process. Being prepared also gives you more confidence to explore if the company is right for you as well.

I believe the right job for you is out there and using the information here along with the tools in the tool book and action planner and appendices in this book will help you find it.

Good luck!

Ellyn

When they finally get you on the phone, what helps?

Level of energy and tone, not saying "like" or "you know" after every third word. The ability to articulate. I'm looking for someone who expresses interest in the company. Someone who says, "I am really interested in your company. I have researched and you are doing some exciting things. I studied your website."

I want your five-second story: "I just graduated from Syracuse with a degree in Communications, I've had some internships the last few summers, I'm really excited about your company, you are leaders in the market, you have a solid reputation, and I would love to meet with you." That's it. It's a story and although it's five seconds, in that story you have told me a touch about you, a touch about my company and you have conveyed your energy and enthusiasm. That's all I need.

**Human Resources Associate,
global public relations firm**

Appendices

If a candidate misses the campus interview, how do they get your attention?

It depends on why they missed the campus interview and I want to know why. Sometimes they have a good reason and can't be there. Email me your resume and follow it up with a phone call.

But you must have a great reason why you didn't make the campus interview.

**Human Resources Officer,
Big Four accounting firm**

What are some surefire mistakes?

Being overly aggressive or cocky is a turn off. Confidence is different than cocky and overly aggressive.

How can a candidate get your attention?

Through a connection.

What about attire?

Don't overdress but dress professional. Even though we are more casual, a suit is not over dressing.

How important are internships?

They really help. It shows me they have experience other than school projects.

Advice for grads?

Interview a lot to get some practice. Get out there and try it. Talk to a lot of people.

Take some summer jobs and internships.

**Controller,
law practice industry**

Appendix 1:
Sample Tables

(To add rows—in Word, highlight a row and then go to "Table." You can insert a row above or below)

JOB DESCRIPTION INTERVIEW PREP TOOL

EMPLOYER NEEDS	WHAT I HAVE	STORY	STORY DETAILS

SAMPLE: JOB DESCRIPTION INTERVIEW PREP TOOL

EMPLOYER NEEDS	WHAT I HAVE	STORY	STORY DETAILS
Microsoft Access skills	2 years in office using Access	Making a new database of customers	We increased mailing effectiveness by 20% when I created a master client list in Access, and experienced fewer returned mail pieces.

Copyright © 2010 EKS Consultants, Inc.

Appendix 2:
60 Possible Interview Questions

Here is a sample of 60 questions to practice with.
Remember, read the job description, think of the purpose behind the question, and match your story to the purpose.

1. Tell me about a time when you were a member of a great team. What role did you play in making the team great?

2. Tell me about a time when you were given a task to accomplish without any direction.

3. Tell me about a time when you had to work with someone you did not get along with.

4. Tell me about a time when you felt that a decision was unfair. How did you handle it?

5. Tell me about a time when someone asked you for assistance outside the parameters of your job. What did you do?

6. Tell me about a time you had to multitask.

7. Tell me about a time when you were creative in solving a problem.

8. Tell me about a time when you were the leader of a team and the team disagreed with your decision. How did you handle it?

9. Tell me about a time when you were a team leader and had to mediate with members who disagreed with each other.

10. Tell me about a project that did not go well.

11. Tell me about a time that you worked hard to accomplish something but didn't.

12. Tell me about a time when you suggested a better way to do something.

13. Tell me about a time when you had to handle conflict within your group.

14. You are a team member and you disagree with an important decision that you believe will have a negative impact on the project. How will you proceed?

15. Tell me about a time when someone told you that you had made an error. Describe how you would react and what you would say in your defense.

16. You are a new employee at our firm and I have asked you to speak to a group of 10 employees. What would you talk about and what would you say?

17. You are part of a team working on a project with a one-week deadline. The team leader does not seem to be on top of things and you are worried about reaching the deadline. What do you do?

18. How do you handle a crisis? Describe one that you handled well.

19. Describe one that you didn't handle well and what you would have done differently.

20. It's five o'clock on Friday and your supervisor gives you an assignment that needs to be finished by 8:00 am Monday morning. You have plans to be away for the weekend. What do you do?

21. Describe a situation that was a great learning experience.

22. Describe a challenge you faced in school and how you handled it.

23. Describe an experience that you felt was rewarding.

24. Describe a situation where you were mentored.

25. Describe a situation where you were given feedback on your performance that wasn't what you had hoped for.

26. Describe a situation where you resolved a problem.

27. What would your last boss/manager say about you?

28. How would your co-workers describe you?

29. What do you think is the best part of working in teams?

30. What do you think is the worst part of working in a team?

31. How do you define "work ethic"? How would you describe yours?

32. How do you make decisions?

33. What type of people do you like to work with?

34. What motivates you?

35. Give me 10 adjectives to describe yourself.

36. How do you like to be managed?

37. Tell me about your best manager. Why do you consider them the "best"?

38. Tell me about your worst manager. Why do you consider them the "worst"?

39. What book are you reading now?

40. What books have you read about leadership?

41. Describe your ideal job.

42. What was the most creative thing you have ever done?

43. What are you most proud of?

44. How do handle stress at work?

45. What would you liked to have done more of in your last internship?

46. What would you like to have done less of in your last internship?

47. Why did you choose your last job/internship?

48. Why did you choose your school?

49. If you could have done anything different during your college career, what would it have been?

50. What are your short- and long-term career goals?

51. In what areas would you like to develop further?

52. What skills did it take to succeed in your internships?

53. What do you know about our company?

54. What makes you the best candidate?

55. Why should we hire you?

56. What made you apply for this job?

57. Where else are you interviewing?

58. How would you describe client satisfaction?

59. What do you think is most important in great customer service?

60. What will you do if you don't get this job?

Appendix 3:
Legal and Illegal Interview Questions

State and federal laws make discrimination in certain protected categories illegal. These categories are:

Race	Marital status	Religion
Color	Childcare	Illness
Sex	Family status	Sexual orientation
Age	National origin	Pregnancy status
Disability		

Acceptable areas of questioning include:

Education

Skills

Prior employment

General questions related to the job description regarding:

    Goals

    Strengths

    Weaknesses

    Other characteristics mentioned in the job description

I don't believe that most employers ask an illegal question on purpose. I do believe when they ask an illegal question it is because they do not know any better. That being said, do you want to work for an employer who does not know the law?

In some cases, such as a start-up, the employer may not have an HR person and therefore may not know how to conduct a proper interview.

Either way the most important point here is to remember that there is a purpose behind every interview question.

If you are asked an illegal question you have several choices on how to answer:

First, think about what the purpose of the question might be. For example, say an interviewer asks you if you have young children. That is an illegal question, but what could be the purpose? Perhaps there is a lot of overnight travel in the position and the interviewer wants to make sure the candidate can commit to the travel required. Of course, what the interviewer should do is to describe in detail the travel required, how often, where, and the time commitment and ask the candidate if he/she is willing to do that and capable of making the commitment. But if the interviewer asks the illegal question, here are some choices.

1. **You can choose to answer.**
   By doing this you might help your chances of getting the job—if you give the right answer. However, lying is never acceptable. Always tell the truth.

2. **You can refuse to answer.**
   You can simply say that this is an illegal question and that you prefer not to answer it. The interviewer may, however, see you as confrontational.

3. **You can let the interviewer know that you know this is an illegal question** and ask what it is they need to know and why.

In the example used above, you might respond: *"As I'm sure you know, questions about children are illegal. But if you would share with me why you are asking, perhaps I can give you some information that would help you in your decision process."* If the interviewer then says that he/she wants to make sure you can do the travel, you might then say, *"I can assure you that I am able and willing to commit to the travel requirements of the position."*

It's okay to let the interviewer know that you know the law. It shows your knowledge.

4. **You can ask how the question relates to the job requirements.**

Similar to the above, this response keeps the interviewer focused on the job description.

If the employer insists on pursuing this type of questioning and the above doesn't work, then you should end the interview by telling the interviewer that you are not interested in the position.

Job Descriptions and How to Interpret Them

Appendix 4:
Job Description Example #1

Job Snapshot from internet job board

Location:	Greenwich Village, NYC, NY 10014
Employee Type:	Full-Time
Industry:	Fashion—Apparel—Textile
	Public Relations
	Sales—Marketing
Manages Others:	No
Job Type:	Marketing
	Sales
	Professional Services
Experience:	Not Specified
Travel:	Negligible
Post Date:	1/14/2010

Contact
Information:
Ref ID: Public Relations

Description

Public Relations and Promotional Marketing Intern—Jewelry—Fashion.

We are a privately held jewelry wholesaler headquartered in New York. We cater primarily to large department stores and major jewelry store chains.

Overview

The ideal candidate will be responsible for growing the site's social media network—creating viral exposure of the site on targeted networks/blogs and forums—creating links and partnerships with other sites and work in a team on SEO efforts for the site.

No experience required, as we will train the ideal candidate.

Key Responsibilities

* To visit and source blogs relating to popular jewelry trends.
* Be able to communicate with individuals in a professional/friendly manner.
* Overall grow the exposure of companyname.com.

Requirements

- Public Relations and Promotional Marketing Intern —Jewelry—Fashion
- Bachelor's degree in fields that emphasize communications (Sales,Marketing, Public Relations, English, Journalism, etc.).
- Interest in Internet social networking.
- Experience with blogs/blogging desired.
- Basic copywriting skills preferred.
- Must have excellent written, verbal communication and language skills.

Skills Learned on the Job

- Search Engine Optimization
- Marketing

How to Interpret the Job Description

Black = Knowledge, **Gray = Skills**, Light Gray = Soft Skills

Job Snapshot

Location: Greenwich Village, NYC, NY 10014

If you are in another state or city for school and are planning to move back home to NYC then your resume should have your home address in New York on it.

Employee Type: Full-Time

Industry: ***Fashion—Apparel—Textile***

Public Relations

Sales—Marketing: You will be asked about your knowledge of these industries—Incorporate your knowledge of these industries in your seven stories.

Manages Others: No

Job Type: Marketing

Sales

Professional Services

Experience: Not Specified

Travel: Negligible

Post Date: 1/14/2010

Contact
Information
Ref ID: Public Relations

Description

Public Relations and Promotional Marketing Intern—Jewelry—Fashion

We are a privately held jewelry wholesaler headquartered in New York. We cater primarily to large department stores and major jewelry store chains.

Overview

The *ideal* candidate will be responsible for growing the site's social media network—creating viral exposure of the site on targeted networks/blogs and forums—creating links and partnerships with other sites and work in a team on SEO efforts for the site.

This tells you the skills you need and you will need to have stories that show your skill at doing this. Notice that it says "Ideal Candidate". This tells you that you do not need all this experience or a great deal of this experience, so some knowledge and experience will be good.

Your resume should reflect/mention any experience you have in these areas. If you do not have any experience in these areas, think about the skills it would take to do this job.

For example: If I were recruiting for this job, I would want someone who is organized and has done Internet research before. Or research in general. I might also want someone who has worked in a large department store and preferably in the jewelry department. Other skills I might look for were excel, problem-solving, resourcefulness, and a sense of urgency. The last two are what I would call soft skills. Make sure your experience and bullets on your resume include evidence of the above.

No experience required, as we will train the ideal candidate.

So no experience is required but if you can show on your resume how you have skills that would help you do well in the position that gives you an edge.

Use this to prepare your job description tool.

Key Responsibilities

- To visit and source blogs relating to popular jewelry trends.
- Be able to communicate with individuals on a professional/friendly manner.

You will get questions on your ability to communicate with people. This is where you might hear "Tell me about a time when you had to handle a difficult customer" These questions will be behavior based and/or situational, such as "Its your first week at your job and you are asked to do some quick research on a website and present your findings to the executive committee. They are the most senior people in the company. How would you proceed?"

Perhaps you don't visit any jewelry blogs. You will want to prepare ahead of time by researching as many as you can find who compete with this company and look at the major department stores jewelry pages online.

Because you don't need experience for this position, the company will be interested in your ability to navigate the web and they will also be interested in your knowledge of blogging. This should be evident in your stories.

- Overall grow the exposure of companyname.com.

Requirements

Public Relations and Promotional Marketing Intern—Jewelry—Fashion

* **Bachelor's degree in fields that emphasize communications (Sales, Marketing, Public Relations, English, Journalism, etc.).**
* Interest in Internet social networking. *The company will check for your presence on Facebook, LinkedIn, Myspace, etc. CLEAN UP YOUR PAGE!!*
* Experience with blogs/blogging desired.
* Basic copywriting skills preferred. *You will most likely be asked for a writing sample and should have some with you.*
* Must have excellent written, verbal communication and language skills. *This you will demonstrate in the interview. The interviewer will evaluate how you engage with them and relate to them.*

Skills Learned on the Job

* Search Engine Optimization
* Marketing

Appendix 5:
Job Description Example #2
Human Resources Intern
Taken From web job board

This position supports the HR compliance and Employee Relations Team. In addition to working with the Director and Managers of Diversity & Inclusion, the successful candidate will work closely with other teams, including EEO, Data Management, Staffing and Compensation, Employee Relations, and Managers.

The responsibilities of this position are as follows:
* Coordinate multiple, parallel projects using formal project planning techniques;
* Research HR best practices (i.e., initiatives and programs) to enhance the delivery of services;
* Responsible for on site logistics and program coordination;
* Assist with benchmarking.

All applicants for this position must be authorized to work in the United States now and in the future without requiring sponsorship.

Job Requirements

* Required to be enrolled in a bachelor's degree program and to be a junior or senior, or enrolled in a master's degree program.
* Candidates pursuing a degree in business, human resources or minority studies preferred.

Experience Requirements:

* Demonstrated analytical and project management skills
* Strong proficiency with computer programs (Excel, Word, PowerPoint)
* Excellent verbal and written communications skills
* Solutions oriented, with an emphasis on creativity and diligence
* Demonstrated ability to work with time sensitive and confidential information

How to Interpret the Job Description

Black = Knowledge, **Gray = Skills**, *Light Gray = Soft Skills*

This position *supports* the HR compliance and Employee Relations Team. In addition to working with the Director and Managers of Diversity & Inclusion, the successful candidate will *work closely with other teams*, including EEO, Data Management, Staffing and Compensation, Employee Relations and Managers. (EEO stands for Equal Employment Opportunity. If you see terms, such as EEO, in a job description that you do not understand, google it and find out what it is.)

This is a supportive role so your participation in team projects as a team member, not necessarily team leader, in school or elsewhere is important for your seven stories.

Also, your knowledge of diversity, and EEO will be helpful. If you don't feel confident do some homework and research the topics on the Internet. Check the company website for info as well.

The responsibilities of this position are as follows:

* Coordinate multiple, parallel projects using formal project planning techniques;

  Examples in your seven stories.

* Research HR best practices (i.e., initiatives and programs) to enhance the delivery of services;

  When have you researched something which re-

sulted in achievement of a goal or improvement of something.

* Responsible for on site logistics and program coordination.

Examples of how you coordinated efforts of others to accomplish a task or goal in your stories.

* Assist with benchmarking.

This is more of an analytical skill, but you should know what benchmarking is and give an example of how you have worked with it or something similar before.

All applicants for this position must be authorized to work in the United States now and in the future without requiring sponsorship.

Job Requirements

* **Required to be enrolled in a bachelor's degree program and to be a junior or senior, or enrolled in a master's degree program.**
* **Candidates pursuing a degree in business, human resources or minority studies preferred.**

Experience Requirements

* Demonstrated analytical and project management skills.

Examples of your project leadership and your ability to analyze and solve a problem.

* Strong proficiency with computer programs (Excel, Word, PowerPoint).

Examples of reports, PowerPoint presentations, etc that fit with the job description, if you have them but remember to leave off confidential information.

* Excellent verbal and written communications skills

You will demonstrate this in the interview

* Solutions-oriented, with an emphasis on creativity and diligence.

Stories of how you have come up with solutions to problems or challenges, preferably ones that were creative and that required persistence.

* Demonstrated ability to work with time-sensitive and confidential information.

Examples of how you have been trusted with proprietary information and can maintain confidentiality. Also stories of how you made deadlines.

JOB DESCRIPTION # 2 INTERVIEW PREP TOOL
HUMAN RESOURCES INTERNSHIP

EMPLOYER NEEDS	WHAT I HAVE	STORY	STORY DETAILS
Proficiency with computer programs	Excel, PowerPoint, Word	Employee awards program	Created PowerPoint proposal for employee awards program and presented it to senior management. Was told how creative and well done it was. Have example of it with me with anything confidential left off
Solutions oriented/ creativity and diligence	Redesigned and shortened exit interview spread sheet	When I realized the spreadsheet could be shortened for efficiency	I went to my supervisor with the proposal to redesign the spreadsheet. Example of before and after without confidentiality

Copyright © 2010 EKS Consultants, Inc.

Appendix 6:
Job Description Example #3

This is a partial example of a job description from a top-tier management consulting firm. The post is from their website which includes a lot more information about the company, its mission, vision, values, and most importantly, their expectations of their new hires. It also includes a very detailed description of what candidates will experience. You must make sure to read all parts of the careers section on the company website to gather clues of what you will be asked in the interview. For example, if the information says the learning curve is challenging and steep, you should expect to answer questions regarding how you handled challenging problems and a burden of learning quickly. You should be prepared with this evidence in your seven stories.

In reading below, if I were interviewing a candidate for this position, I would simply ask, *"Tell me about a time when your creativity was the most important asset in a team project."* Because this is a management consulting firm you would definitely have a case interview.

Job description:

We are seeking exceptional candidates who are **seniors at a select number of colleges and universities.** Candidates from **all academic majors are encouraged to apply.**

To qualify for our Business Analyst program, you should possess the following:

- **Undergraduate degree**
- **Strong academic performance: 3.5 cumulative GPA (minimum) strongly preferred**
- **Superior analytical and problem-solving skills**
- **Effective interpersonal and communication skills**
- **Demonstrated leadership and team-building abilities**
- **Creativity, self-confidence, and flexibility**
- **An intent to pursue an MBA degree**
- **Willingness to travel (required)**

The above is more of the same. However, expect to get a case interview here and most likely more than one. Your stories should have concrete examples of how you exhibited each of the requirements above.

JOB DESCRIPTION # 3 INTERVIEW PREP TOOL
MANAGEMENT CONSULTING

EMPLOYER NEEDS	WHAT I HAVE	STORY	STORY DETAILS
Cumulative GPA 3.5	GPA 3.8	Honors Deans List	Worked part-time to pay expenses
Effective interpersonal and communication skills	Excellent Public speaking skills Excellent negotiating skills	Debate club Resolved client conflicts	Won debate competition Communicated with Controller of Client XYZ to resolve billing issues
Demonstrated Leadership	President of Fraternity	Chaired annual fundraising event	Led team of 35 fundraisers to achieve highest dollars raised
Creativity and flexibility	Idea generator Incorporates others ideas	Developed idea for new product for case project Worked with the team to refine and improve product	Developed the ABC product idea and took it to the team who gave some constructive feedback. Wasn't easy to hear criticism but they were right and together we refined it and developed a better product

This tool should be used for every job you interview for. The story details box is an abbreviated version of your story, from you 7 stories.

The Tool Book and Action Guide
The toolbook and action guide provides more indepth preparation and study.

It includes the self assessment and discovery tool that is the foundation for your 7 stories, 30 second commercial, discovery of your strengths and weaknesses, and tools for preparing them and articulating them in an interview. In addition you will find:

More before and after resumes
Information on Networking
Job Search Strategy tips
Assessment and discovery interpretation
Additional Tool sheet examples filled out
Cover letter examples
Thank you note examples
And More...

To order the toolbook, go to www.jobinterviewskills101.com or www.collegetocareercoaching.com.

Appendix 7:
Your 30 Second Commercial

The 30 second commercial is a simple and concise answer to the interview question, "Tell me about yourself." This ambiguous question is a great opportunity to pass key information about you to the interviewer. Your answer is an overview of you. You want to write this out and when you put it all together memorize it and say it in the mirror 100 times. Keep in mind that you want to include information about you and your experiences that relates to the job description. Once you have it down practice saying it so it sounds unrehearsed. From the prospective of the candidate, this is a feared question, but will inevitably come up in a first round interview so preparation is key.

The first step to crafting a response is breaking the question down into more specific parts. The main ideas in this question are:

- Who are you?
    Key points—Background, schooling

- What have you done? (what do you bring to the position)
    Key points—Relevant jobs/internships, volunteer work, travels, other experiences

- What are your strengths?
  Look at the job description—what strengths would you need to have to do well in the job. If you have them say so here and have stories to prove it.

- What are you looking for?
  Key points—Desired position and future expectations of position.

The second step is fitting all of the information pertaining to these questions into only 30 seconds. This is challenging, but with practice anything is possible.

Now, answer the three questions separately. Make sure you touch upon the key points. The space for writing your responses is short because your answers should be short. Here are some tips before you begin.

- Cut out the superlatives
- Be unique
- Say what you need to say not what you think the interviewer wants to hear and be truthful

Who are you?

_____

_____

_____

_____

_____

What have you done?

_____

_____

_____

_____

_____

What are your strengths?

_____

_____

_____

_____

_____

What are you looking for?

_____

_____

_____

_____

_____

Revise and fine tune your responses so they flow together. Have a friend listen to you say it.